I F A W I N E W E
WHICH WOULD IT B

FOREWORD — 9

INTRODUCTION — 10

THE HISTORICAL RELATIONSHIP OF PEOPLE AND WINES — 11

SIMILARITIES BETWEEN PEOPLE and WINES — 11

GRAPE CHARACTERISTICS IN GENERAL — 13

WINE MAKING & BASIC DIFFERENCES — 13

GENERAL GRAPE VARIETIES — 14

OLD WORLD VS. NEW WORLD PHILOSOPHY — 14

BWINE PERSONALITY CHART (abbreviated concept from Bwinedate.com) — 15

BASIC CHARACTERISTICS — 16

WINE STRUCTURAL CHARACTERISTICS — 16

WINE EXPRESSION — 17

WINE STYLE (TASTE)- FLAVOR PROFILES — 18

WINE CONCLUSION - FINISH — 19

SO HERE WE ARE... — 20

I F A W I N E W E R E M E . . .
WHICH WOULD IT BE?

WINE SPEAK - WHITE — 21

WHITE GRAPE VARIETALS — 21

VINIFICATION — 21

VITICULTURE — 22

ALBARINO — 23

CHARDONNAY — 24

WHITE VARIETAL FEATURE - CHARDONNAY / GARY FARRELL — 26

CHENIN BLANC / STEEN — 29

FRIULANO — 30

WHITE VARIETAL FEATURE - FRIULANO / TENUTE TOMASELLA — 31

GARGANEGA - (MOST REFER TO AS SOAVE - REGION WHERE IT IS PRIMARILY GROWN) — 34

GEWÜRZTRAMINER — 35

GRÜNER VELTLINER — 36

MUSCADELLE - (NOT TO BE CONFUSED WITH MUSCAT OR MUSCADET) — 37

PINOT GRIS / PINOT GRIGIO — 38

RIBOLLA GIALLA — 39

IF A WINE WERE ME . . .

WHICH WOULD IT BE?

WHITE VARIETAL FEATURE - RIBOLLA GIALLA / LIVON, RONCALTO   41

RIESLING   44

WHITE VARIETAL FEATURE - RIESLING / EFESTĒ   46

SAUVIGNON BLANC / FUME BLANC   49

SEMILLON   50

TORRONTES   51

VIOGNIER   53

WHITE VARIETAL FEATURE - VIOGNIER / CINDER   54

WINE SPEAK - RED   57

RED / BLACK GRAPE VARIETIES   57

VINIFICATION   57

VITICULTURE   58

AGLIANICO   59

BRUNELLO (DI MONTALCINO) - clone of SANGIOVESE   60

CABERNET FRANC   61

RED VARIETAL FEATURE - CABERNET FRANC / BARBOURSVILLE   62

IF A WINE WERE ME . . .

WHICH WOULD IT BE?

CABERNET SAUVIGNON   64

CARMENERE   66

CINSAULT   67

GAMAY   68

GRENACHE/GARNACHA   69

MALBEC / AUXERROIS   70

RED VARIETAL FEATURE - MALBEC / FINCA DECERO   72

MERLOT   74

RED VARIETAL FEATURE - MERLOT / BENZIGER   75

MONTEPULCIANO   77

NEBBIOLO (BAROLO, BARBARESCO)   78

PINOT NOIR   80

RED VARIETAL FEATURE - PINOT NOIR / DAVIS FAMILY   82

SANGIOVESE (CHIANTI, BRUNELLO AND VINO NOBILE)   85

SYRAH / SHIRAZ   86

TEMPRANILLO   88

IF A WINE WERE ME . . .
WHICH WOULD IT BE?

RED VARIETAL FEATURE - TEMPRANILLO / TEMPUS ALBA   89

ZINFANDEL / PRIMITIVO   91

BLENDING: REDS BENEFIT FROM WHITES   92

WINE SPEAK - SPARKLING   93

SPARKLING WINES   94

STYLES OF SPARKLING WINES   96

SPARKLING WINE FEATURE - Osè Rosé / TENUTE TOMASELLA   101

WINE SPEAK - DESSERT   108

DESSERT WINES - FORTIFIED / NON-FORTIFIED   109

DESSERT / FORTIFIED WINES   111

FORTIFIED WINES   112

MADEIRA   113

FORTIFIED WINE FEATURE - MADEIRA / THE RARE WINE CO & BARBEITO   114

PORTS   117

FORTIFIED WINE FEATURE - PORT / SANDEMAN   118

SHERRY   121

I F A W I N E W E R E M E . . .
WHICH WOULD IT BE?

VINS DOUX NATURELS / VDN   122

VIN DE LIQUEUR   123

FORTIFIED WINE FEATURE - VIN DE LIQUEUR / KARANTES   124

NON-FORTIFIED WINES   125

SAUTERNES / LOUPIAC   126

TOKAJI ASZU   127

VIN SANTO   128

EISWEIN / ICEWINE   129

IN CONCLUSION   130

WINE PROFILE ASSESSMENT   131

ACKNOWLEDGEMENTS   132

NOTEWORTHY CREDITS FOR BOOK   133

LaSaan Georgeson

IF A WINE WERE ME...WHICH WOULD IT BE?

BOLD - SEXY - BUBBLY - SWEET

Edited by Jennifer Chhatlani

Cover art by Peter Georgeson

self published and updated / October 2013

IF A WINE WERE ME...WHICH WOULD IT BE?

From the creator of Bwinedate.com

~ | ~

WINES ARE ORGANIC, WITH INHERENT CHARACTERISTICS

JUST LIKE YOU AND ME!

READ ON TO LEARN THEIR

ATTRIBUTES, PERSONALITIES, STYLES AND FINISHES.

THEN, DETERMINE WHICH VARIETAL OR STYLE IS MORE AKIN TO YOU

RED, WHITE, SPARKLING, OR DESSERT

THIS BOOK WAS PRODUCED FOR YOU AND YOUR BAR COUNTER... CHEERS!

FOREWORD

Before you begin, you should know that I am a consummate dreamer and believer; not much, if anything, holds me down because I continually live my life with hope and passion, choosing only to see opportunities - not obstacles. When a door is boarded up without access I am the one that spots the nearby window as an entry point.

A few years ago, my tightly structured life really started to spin out of control. It unraveled into messy pieces, then to only ravel again with less structure. I had recently purchased a condo after moving to a new city while the dislike for my-then career was growing ever stronger, largely due to higher level executives than me who had little regard for investing in their employees. They only saw the poor economic climate (as well as me) as a threat, and many of my friends and colleagues were starting to feel the struggle of the economy. To top it off, I lost my dearest friend in the world, my mother (Clara Green). Ugh! In my mind it quickly became clear that I had just a few choices: stay where I was, where sorrow and misery might consume me, quickly find another job just to satisfy my income needs, or find a way to reinvent my life and start living it with the enjoyment and abundant intentions in the way that I used to. Of course I took the latter route and have not looked back. This book is one of the many outcomes of reinventing my life and living it with appreciation and purpose.

WHY a book about the personalities of wines...am I kidding? Not at all! My intention in creating this book is both about having some real fun with wines as well as making wine knowledge more approachable. While I have completely reinvented my career, becoming a Sommelier, I have not lost the joy in seeing people learn new things and gain confidence during that journey. There will be no tests afterwards, but I do hope you get a few chuckles while you learn some tidbits about wine varietals.

My hope is that you discover something new about wines and their diverse personalities; perhaps you will even discover something about yourself! When you are done, be sure to check out the services idea behind the book at www.bwinedate.com. It is sure to create fun times!

In the meantime….Cheers.

WHICH WOULD IT BE?

INTRODUCTION

If A Wine Were Me.... is simply a fun way to highlight the similarities of wine to living, organic species; essentially, wine varietals personified. When I speak of 'me' in the title, I want you to consider the characteristics of the myriad of grape varieties in determining which one or two resonates with your own attributes. The most enjoyable part of the book, particularly for you Wine-O's (Wine Optimists) is that you will start to understand wines from a personalized perspective. Certainly a much easier way to remember the varietal distinctions!

While reading, discover whether one variety feels more like your personality than another based on your mood. Does it change? Can you identify what wine elements would balance your personality? Is your personality a blend of varieties? If so, which ones, and what are the main characteristics suggesting a blend?

If you are more daring, grab a friend to help you determine which variety best represents your specific personality...and find out which of your friends knows you better. And for the foodies, the book offers up basic food suggestions for which your wine persona might best pair.

I sincerely hope you enjoy the witty nature of the book as much as I enjoyed writing it~

LaSaan Georgeson

WHICH WOULD IT BE?

THE HISTORICAL RELATIONSHIP OF PEOPLE AND WINES

Since practically the beginning of time, people and wines have had a history together; whether for spiritual ceremonies, social celebrations, or healing purposes, this relationship between Wines and People has existed for centuries.

Wines date back at the least to the 5th - 6th century B.C. when there was a place in the world actually called Transcaucasia. During that time, wines had a spiritual purpose and provided healing remedies with Gods like Dionysis and Bacchus. Alcohol was much safer to drink than water, and was used as a treatment for several ailments.

As civilizations progressed, wines were further defined through religion; the monks that made the drink were largely responsible for many of the esteemed practices used in winemaking today. They kept copious documents to define the standards and consistencies of winemaking. You may have heard of one of the more famous monks, Dom Perignon, who is known for his thumbprint on winemaking methods and for whom a fine Champagne is named after.

SIMILARITIES BETWEEN PEOPLE and WINES

Now that you've read about the brief historically steeped relationship of the two, we can begin to draw out some of the similarities. There are different vine species, namely three, and when it comes to the species of vines, we are only discussing one - Vitis Vinifera. And, with all of the different mammals in the world we will only focus on one - humans.

There is a great amount of diversity within these two species. Vitis Vinifera has easily 10,000 grape varieties in the world--according to Wikipedia that is the population size of the entire Island Country, Republic of Nauru in the South Pacific. There are a little over 31,000 times that amount - approximately 313 million - of people in the United States alone.

While it may be obvious that wines are made from grapes, you may not realize that vine care and careful management is needed for wines to best express their inherent characteristics. Grape vines have a necessary dormancy period during the winter and a growth cycle generally from early spring to fall; the proper management of the periods of rest and growth are critical for success in ripening! Clearly this is not too different for people; many are living testimonials of well-adjusted adults due to proper care and management from infancy to adulthood.

The need to have a winemaker to make wines out of grapes is clear; however, you may not know that creativity and passion is paramount for developing different styles encouraged by the natural characteristics of the variety. There is just as much talent and skill needed to rear a child into an adult.

As you begin the journey into this book, see if you notice any correlation between a wine varietal expression and your personality or maybe the personality of those you know.

I F   A   W I N E   W E R E   M E . . .
WHICH WOULD IT BE?

GRAPE CHARACTERISTICS IN GENERAL

Grapes have a cellular system, as do humans. Grapes derive their DNA (characteristics) from genetic reproduction as do we; however, grapevines are commonly reproduced through designed selection (as in cloning, hybrids, crossing, etc). Grape characteristics are based on the type of variety; and influenced by how the vine growth is managed, and environmental factors such as climate, temperature, sunlight, oxygen, and H_2O; nutrition, soil type, etc. The flavors that we taste in our wines are due in part to these factors.

Consider for a moment that you are a white variety like Sauvignon Blanc, growing up in a cold climate with potential frost issues; however. exposed to reduced amount of sunlight so you will ripen minimally (make it through childhood fine) but your ability to reach a high degree of ripeness (a matured adult) before being picked is diminished. The result of these environmental factors (cool climate, shortened growing season, etc) will be a higher acidic grape (less conversion of acids into sugars) and lower sweetness (less ripening provides less sugar to convert into alcohol).

WINE MAKING & BASIC DIFFERENCES

Making wine is where the spotlight shifts to the winemakers. In the simplest terms, they make "drinkable art" out of raw materials; basically combining the grape pulp with strains of yeast creating alcohol and CO_2. Given the simplified description of the winemaking process,it may be evident that the winemakers ability and techniques (vessels used, length of fermentation, use of oak, etc.) has a direct and significant effect on the final product. You might equate the winemakers' influence on grapes to that of a Professor who has received a student sent to their university or college, returning them to society having blossomed into a perfectly polished (or, in some cases, not so polished) Being.

The wine's **style** (dry, off-dry, medium-dry, sparkling, sweet, rosé) is dependent on the winemaker's choice as well.

The simplest difference in making red wines vs. white wines is that red wines are allowed to macerate on their skins during the process (creating more complexity with the different hues that we see in a wine glass) while the white wines generally do not. If so, there is limited time macerating on the skins for some varietals and/or styles - they strive to keep clarity with slight color subtleties seen in the glass. Overall, it is necessary to provide for and care for grapevines; requires the viticulturist attention to ensure the vines are maintained and that the soil is ideal for the particular variety, etc. Equally important is vinification (the process of making wine from raw materials) with intentional distinction requiring craftsmanship of the winemaker.

I F   A   W I N E   W E R E   M E . . .

WHICH WOULD IT BE?

GENERAL GRAPE VARIETIES

Of the myriad varieties, there are some commonly known and grown International types that I will mention. White varieties: Chardonnay, Pinot Gris, Riesling, Sauvignon Blanc and Viognier, and red varieties: Cabernet Sauvignon, Grenache, Merlot, Pinot Noir, and Sangiovese. Each has their own distinctions or personalities based on where they are grown (brought up).

OLD WORLD VS. NEW WORLD PHILOSOPHY

Old world wines generally refer to those from European countries steeped in tradition and providing true representations of a sense of the place in which they are grown, called terroir. This includes influences like soil type, climate, aspect, heart and soul of the winemaker, etc., and being less fruit-forward. However, wines of the New world made in North & South America, New Zealand, Australia, South Africa have been known to be more fruit-forward and technology driven/ less about where they are grown. However with all the sharing of knowledge and practices between the old and new world wines and adapting to consumers palate interests, it can be a challenge to *distinguish* the taste from either style. But then too, that doesn't matter much for this book only to say that if you want to know which philosophy of wine most resembles you/your personality (old vs. new) then good on you!

I F   A   W I N E   W E R E   M E . . .

BWINE PERSONALITY CHART (abbreviated concept from Bwinedate.com)

WINES	HUMAN BEINGS
BASIC CHARACTERISTICS	INHERENT ATTRIBUTES
EXPRESSIONS	PERSONALITY
STYLE	STYLE
FINISH	DEMEANOR

The chart above represents the correlation between wine varietals and humans. When looking at the Wine side of the chart, consider the characteristics of a grape varietal, such as how it is vinified and expressed as a wine, the varying styles derived from this expression, and finishing with the taste we experience in the glass.

When you look at the Human side of the chart, think about the inherent attributes that all of us are born with, how our development shapes our personalities, which then help define the style or taste that we become known as, and how all of this concludes with our overall demeanor.

- Basic Characteristics of a grape = Inherent Attributes of an individual

- Expression of the wine from the grape = Personality of an individual

- Style of the wine = Style or taste of an individual

- Finish of the wine = Demeanor or disposition of an individual

Further context and visuals are provided on the following pages to further depict the connection between wines and human beings.

I F   A   W I N E   W E R E   M E . . .

WHICH WOULD IT BE?

The Characteristics of a wine translates to the Attributes of a person.

BASIC CHARACTERISTICS

This category, described in the charts on the following pages, highlight the grape variety DNA and the resulting wine structure in terms of acids, body, tannins and alcohol.

As you read the descriptions of the different characteristics, you will notice they have been created as attributes to people -- explore likeliness to yours. An individual type, or solo, represents a confident personality that does fine without others whereby a supporting cast is best in the company of others (a blend). Age-ability is also touched upon, representing patience.

WINE STRUCTURAL CHARACTERISTICS

Acids equal excitement, freshness and are *described* in terms of brightness, outgoing attitude, perky, being vocal;
Body is the impression of texture and is *described* as structure and capability to hold up to pressure; secure; etc;
Tannins, mainly for red varieties and a few white ones, is about textural richness and is *indicated* by being. comfortable in their skins, being adorned by oak, gum drying, firm and robust;
Alcohol mostly displayed in the finish is closely aligned to the body and described as weight, sturdiness and boozy.

© Sergey Gavrilichev - Dreaamstime

I F   A   W I N E   W E R E   M E . . .

The Expression of a wine translates to the Personality of a person.

WINE EXPRESSION

This category has been used to give you an idea of the nuances of the grape once it is vinified and, as a human, how might your personality reflect that described as a wine. This includes how well you stand out with aromas; how taste descriptors speak to your expressive (outgoing or timid) nature; the range of traits that represent versatility as a person; and the effect of mixing you with other elements represents your ability to adapt more readily in different situations.

© Ivaleksa - Dreaamstime

The Style of a wine translates to the Style of a person.

WINE STYLE (TASTE)- FLAVOR PROFILES

Information shared about flavor (style) is reflective of a person's style and represents the different points in you rmouth. These points are mostly on your tongue as well the effect on your gums mostly in terms of a drying sensation (from tannins). Sweetness is most often detected on the tip of your tongue; salty / herbaceous or savory and tartness of acids, most often on the sides of your tongue creating a watering experience, bitterness as in tannins reflected often at the back of. your tongue The sensation in your mouth is also described as "mouthfeel", referring to a smooth or velvety nature, an oily or creamy note, or more coarse/rugged nature with astringency.

© Svetlana Zdanchuk - Dreaamstime

I F   A   W I N E   W E R E   M E . . .

WHICH WOULD IT BE?

The Finish of a wine translates to the Demeanor of a person.

WINE CONCLUSION - FINISH

Think about this section as a summary of the wine and how it follows-through representing a person's demeanor. Its length/linger, its engagement level, complexity or simplicity. This represents your easy-going or challenging attributes. Harmonizing notes represent well balanced demeanor, etc. Alcohol is closely aligned with physical texture due to the affect on body of a wine, and can be represented as the fabric or textural aspect of a variety. Age here represents the willingness to hang in there as development grow more interesting.

© Lindwa - Dreaamstime

I F A W I N E W E R E M E . . .
WHICH WOULD IT BE?

SO HERE WE ARE...

As you read through each of the different varietals, consider taking the following journey in your mind with me: You are at a fun social gathering and there is a wide range of individuals from different backgrounds - some are mingling and others not. Perhaps there is some really cool energizing music playing in the background, which catches your attention as it bounces off the high loft-like ceilings with warm lights creating small bubbles on the walls and contributing to the overall vibe. Clearly there must be some interest and intrigue with the diverse group of people reflected, whether plain and simple; bold and outspoken; fashionably cheeky, or reserved and quiet.

Now I want you to envision that each of them represents a glass of wine (you included, of course). Which of the glass(es) of wines seem more akin to your attributes? Personality? Style? Demeanor? Why? Which of the other varietals seem interesting to you? What would you do to give them a try?

Now let's start the journey of assessment, at least over the next several chapters, and see where it takes you.... Consider completing the profile at the end of the book if that helps you move forward.

WINE SPEAK - WHITE

WHITE GRAPE VARIETALS

Generally speaking, white varieties tend to have a higher level of acidity (think lemons) creating a zesty and fresh experience. As you read about the white varieties, consider the way in which they are grown and produced as well as the traits of each variety in helping to determine which one speaks to your personality. Keep in mind, you may find that a blend of varieties speak more to your personality than a single variety.

VINIFICATION

This is the process of making grapes into wines by the winemaker. In the case of white wines, the winemaker has several choices to deliver the final product: choose to have some skin contact, as with Reds, to increase the degree of flavors; allow a bit of air interaction to add interest based on the aging vessel chosen; and adjusting the temperature during fermentation to increase the aromatics. These choices will help influence the styles: dry (minimal sweetness), off-dry (slight sweetness) or sweet (completely sweet).

Friulano grape

Friulano bottled

Friulano in a glass, left

I F   A   W I N E   W E R E   M E . . .

VITICULTURE

This is the more scientific aspect of getting grapes in condition to be made into wines. The viticulturist is much like a caretaker (parent) as he/she has responsibility for the grape from inception to vines and through to harvest. He/she also ensures the varieties are fit for the environment; and manages their entire cycle of rest and growth (including proper management of ripeness and vigor) in the vineyard. Think of it like a headmaster in a boarding school getting the adolescent primed and polished for their next steps/stages in life.

Chardonnay

Riesling

Viognier

ALBARINO

CHARACTERISTICS (ATTRIBUTES)	EXPRESSION (PERSONALITIES)	WINE STYLE (STYLE)	FINISH (DEMEANOR)
I'm accustomed to being solo and love my attractive aromatics of luscious ripened fruits; comfortable acids rounding out my structure. I am naturally medium body but can be made full based on my producer.	Best described as balanced with a fresh crisp attitude, lovely prominent fruit pleasantness. You won't find a lot of variation with me as I'm generally a consistently delicious dry drink (no sweetness necessary).	Lovely and balanced with peach and nectarine intensity, some apricot and screaming limes and a soft touch of spice. My usual style is dry (not fortified or off-dry). I am one harmonious experience, discover me.	I continue to resonate in your mouth after a period of time, calling out reminiscence of yummy southern peaches, baking spice and crisp lime/lemon notes. I'm a balanced finish, so don't let my excited acids concern you.

Place of origin is northwestern Spain; also in Chile known as Alvarino. This grape is definitely an aromatic variety of white flowers and ripe peaches, often with apricots maintaining a nice level of acidity and producing medium-full body wines. The finish is super balanced with sweet peaches and citrus of limes.

Food Styles of **Interest**: Wine from this varietal really has no need for company, but if you have, it doesn't matter as this is a well-balanced varietal that will fit any palate with *or* without food. If you have chosen this wine, identify a medium protein food and/or moderately flavored dish to match this balanced yet aromatic varietal. Basic concepts to matching: wine acidity should exceed the food's acidity (this wine has comfortable acids); the wine's residual sweetness should exceed the food's sweetness; and the weight of the food should match that of the wine. Foods to consider: baked poultry, or simmered or poached white fish with oil or light cream sauce; sautéed shrimp with Spanish peppers and rice; casserole of light grains and baked vegetables with herbs;. medium soft cheeses and multigrain crackers.

WHICH WOULD IT BE?

CHARDONNAY

CHARACTERISTICS (ATTRIBUTES)	EXPRESSION (PERSONALITIES)	WINE STYLE (STYLE)	FINISH (DEMEANOR)
Neutral and versatile; Very much an individual and can hold up to whatever you throw my way...go ahead, adorn me with accessories of oak or the pureness of stainless steel; either way I can adapt. Most comfortable in my med to full body; oftentimes lighter med.	Can show up pure in essence or decked out in buttery oak; I come with an easy attitude as I'm hardy and a neutral balance with minimal needs. I am comfortable and confident in my skin. Did you know there are three of us used in traditional Champagne... I'm the only white variety, confident!	Can be rich, buttery, with ripe apples, mango, bananas and vanilla, that's me in Napa California; Complex, aromas of fruit blossoms, subtleties of green apple and apricot completes me in my original skin, Burgundy; Simple, crisp and light of green apples-keeping it fresh--New Zealand style.	I am not easily forgotten no matter what style/taste you decide! You can even hold on to me, as I age just as nicely as I am in my youth...continuing to get more intriguing with time, if you like character.

Place of origin, Burgundy, France; however, this grape is adaptable to many different climates as it is one of the most planted grapes around the world...It is being produced just about everywhere grapes for wines are grown. The grape is best described as neutral and non-aromatic; however, a Chardonnay from a warm to hot climate like Napa or Sonoma will be fuller body on the palate and seemingly more aromatic as it expresses itself with more tropical notes of mango and yellow delicious apples with lower acid and high alcohol. Often fermented in oak barrels, this adds to the texture and weight of the wine. In much colder climates like Northern Burgundy or even Champagne, it will have a lighter body and express more crisp green apple notes suggesting high acid and lower alcohol. The style of these wines is usually fermented in stainless steel keeping the environment anaerobic.

Food Styles of **Interest**: Any and all company will work.with wines of this varietal..though, of course, some work better than others based on the style in which you are indulging. Assuming that you've chosen this wine, identify a heavier protein food and/or a moderate to flavorful dish to match this fuller structured varietal. Basic concepts to matching: wine acidity should exceed the food's acidity; the wine's residual sweetness should exceed the food's sweetness; and the weight of the food should match that of the wine. For the **Oak influenced** style (often Napa), select creamy-based dishes to cut the oak; grilled meats of chicken, tuna or veal; and roasted vegetables and a heavy sauce with pasta. For **Non oak** (Chablis), consider salmon or sea bass with a butter and wine sauce; veal, chicken or tuna; and a Caesar salad with chicken or seafood. For Old World (matured Burgundian style), consider rich creamy dishes to pick up the complexity of tertiary flavors of the wine, grilled meats and seafoods or herb-crusted simmered meats/seafoods, and heavier vegetables of mushrooms and root vegetables

I F   A   W I N E   W E R E   M E . . .

WHITE VARIETAL FEATURE - CHARDONNAY / GARY FARRELL

Why CHARDONNAY?

This varietal is one of the more common varietals and vinified in many different styles, so be careful about saying I'm not a Chardonnay-type person even if you've already tasted plenty from various different regions. The styes of Chardonnay vary greatly. In the featured 2009 **Rochioli Chardonnay** by **Gary Farrell Vineyards**, this can be simplified in a few words **deliciously crisp and elegant**; pleasant fruits and white floral nose; lovely palate of ripe green apple, pear, and tropical fruit, roasted grains and spices, underscored with a stone-like quality and balanced acidity.

The weather patterns allow the grapes to develop full flavor maturity over an extended growing season while retaining their bright, natural acidity (lower sugar content, in some cases oddly enough) due to cool foggy mornings late in the growing season, followed by warm sunny afternoons.

2009, was a longer than usual season and provided the optimal grape ripening conditions for this varietal without exception!

...**Why not!** When I mentioned about all Chardonnay styles not being equal or the same, one prime example as this region in California, Russian River Valley, which can display a completely different style than some parts of Napa county, even though it's also in California.

IF A WINE WERE ME . . .
WHICH WOULD IT BE?

This youthful 2009 Chardonnay is well-integrated and quite scrumptious as of the tasting in 2011; however it will also continue to improve with age. This wine reminds me of a versatile personality, distinct in style full of intellectual conversation that reveals more of itself and its interests the more time you spend exploring what's not so vivid at first.

About **Gary Farrell Winery**...

A 30-year pioneer of the Russian River Valley wine region, Gary Farrell Winery crafts small-lot artisan wines that capture the balance and stylistic elegance of some of the finest vineyard sites in the region, including Rochioli, Bacigalupi, Durell and Hallberg. Gary Farrell is known for small lot Burgundian-styled (more complex and less fruit-forward), varietally expressive and regionally distinctive Russian River Valley Pinot Noir and Chardonnay. Located on Westside Road near Healdsburg in northern Sonoma County, the winery is perched on a hillside offering panoramic views of the forested valley below.

I F   A   W I N E   W E R E   M E . . .

WHICH WOULD IT BE?

The artisan winemaker....

Under the skillful hand of *winemaker* **Theresa Heredia**, whom understands single vineyard wines all too well and provides her hands-on Burgundian perspective as well as extensive experience with cool-climate Pinot Noir, Chardonnay and small-lot wines. Theresa was a Ph.D. candidate in chemistry with an emphasis on enology at U.C. Davis before leaving to follow her calling as a hands-on winemaker. In early 2012 she was named "Winemaker to Watch" by the San Francisco Chronicle, reflecting her interest in wines that offer a pure expression of their vineyard site and her willingness to experiment with different winemaking techniques.

Additional information on the winery is available at www.garyfarrellwinery.com.

All Chardonnay photography provided by Gary Farrell Vineyards & Winery, and photographer, Alan Campbell

I F   A   W I N E   W E R E   M E . . .

CHENIN BLANC / STEEN

CHARACTERISTICS (ATTRIBUTES)	EXPRESSION (PERSONALITIES)	WINE STYLE (STYLE)	FINISH (DEMEANOR)
I'm naturally a neutral flavored grape with nuances being highlighted based on my degree of ripeness. Due to my bold acids, I can age well.	In my youth, I am crisp with fresh fruit scent, a bit of zest along with a stone-like appeal. I am clear about my attitude (acids) and you have to understand this is one of my strongest traits. That said, my acids soften as I age so you for a more subdued essence, give me some years to meld.	My style is quite versatile. When dry, I start out with green apple, some honeydew melon, and bright limes; as I mature, you taste more of my inherent complexities of minerals and dried fruits. My sweet style will balance the boldness of my acids with the tastes of candied tangerines and rich honey.	My finish is just as diverse as my style and in all cases, I will be memorable whether for a brief bright time in my youth or for a nice complex length in my sweet and/ or aged style. Go ahead and explore me.

Place of origin, Loire Valley, France and grown in other regions throughout France and is a neutral variety. It is vinified in a variety of ways, sweet, sparkling and dry based on how long the grape is allowed to ripen.

Chenin Blanc is known as Steen in it's place of origin Coastal, South Africa and has a med-minus body.

Food Styles of **Interest**: All accompaniments work well with wine of this varietal as you may find the conversation extends trying to sort through the traits. If you have chosen this wine in a dry style, identify a light protein food and/or mildly seasoned dishes to match this lighter acidic varietal. Basic concepts to matching: wine acidity should exceed the food's acidity (this can be a highly acidic wine); the wine's residual sweetness should exceed the food's sweetness; and the weight of the food should match that of the wine. Consider light rice or pasta dishes with cream sauces (to break down the acidity); vegetable and herb casseroles; and stews of lighter meats or seafood.

I F   A   W I N E   W E R E   M E . . .

WHICH WOULD IT BE?

FRIULANO

CHARACTERISTICS (ATTRIBUTES)	EXPRESSION (PERSONALITIES)	WINE STYLE (STYLE)	FINISH (DEMEANOR)
I am rare in most places and do quite well solo as I enjoy enticing others with my aromatics of succulent white flowers and pleasant fruits; balanced acids fitting for my medium structure.	I am as good in my youth as well in maturity (just not too old). I am rather zesty with citrus fruits and pear scent, a bit stone-like quality. My acids are a well integrated part of me and keeps my structure balancing out my fruit sweetness. I am all things conversational.	I'm not well known outside of Italy; pleasant and balanced with pear and orange citrus, not overwhelming yet intriguing with nuances to be explored and balanced excitement. My usual style is dry. I am that unique experience, go ahead and explore me.	Not easily forgotten, am I! From beginning to end I provide just the right amount of excitement, yet careful not to overpower the situation. As you spend time with me, you will find I'm quite persuasive leaving you wanting more of me.

Place of origin, most commonly grown and known is in the northeastern region of Italy, Friuli and is an aromatic variety. It is vinified dry. This lovely balance of acidity in this medium body smooth white variety with subtle almonds on the finish.

Friulano is known as Sauvignon Vert in Chile.

Food Styles of **Interest**: Company of any kind works well with this drink, but easy going and enjoyable may be best. If you have chosen wine from this varietal, identify a light protein food and/or mildly seasoned dishes to match this lighter floral varietal. Basic concepts to matching: wine acidity should exceed the food's acidity; the wine's residual sweetness should exceed the food's sweetness; and the weight of the food should match that of the wine. Consider Italian antipasto, cured meats and light pasta dishes; polenta; potato based soups; poultry or white fish simmered with oil or light cream sauces; and Asian cuisine (sushi and/or sashimi).

IF A WINE WERE ME . . .
WHICH WOULD IT BE?

WHITE VARIETAL FEATURE - FRIULANO / TENUTE TOMASELLA

Why FRIULANO?

This varietal is less common in most parts outside of Northeastern Italy and yet is sure to be a rising star with it's vibrant yet structured characteristics of intense floral perfume, almost incense-like; a nutty quality with a beautiful balance of acidity and structure, highlighting a *subtle* fruit sweetness of fresh squeezed mandarin orange and pear.

Definitely meant to be drank young but surprisingly can age a few years while maintaining its acidity (vibrancy).

...Why not!

While attending tastings I have tasted this varietal plenty and my most memorable impression by far is the Friulano from **Tenute Tomasella Winery**... in a couple words, **deliciously exciting**! The expression of this wine showcases a confident personality nicely bundled in a package of finesse while still developing. And feels more like a gorgeously delicate female emanating from a source of no-nonsense power *seeking and discovering*.

Did I mention this Tenute Tomasella **Friulano** wine is the *recipient* of the **Silver medal**, Gilbert & Gallard!

IF A WINE WERE ME . . .

WHICH WOULD IT BE?

Tenute Tomasella

A little info about the winery behind this silver medal winner....

Tenute Tomasella is a second generation family operated winery located in Mansuè on the border between two prestigious wine regions, Friuli Venezia Giulia and Veneto. The change of pace more recently in Mansuè with the further development of the still wine production (like **Friulano**) from the Friuli vineyards and the precision based techniques provides strength to the brand. The philosophy of Tenute Tomasella is that a glass of Tomasella wine embodies not only the art of making wine but the Italian culture as a whole and always focusing on the beautiful side of life "La Dolce Vita".

All Friuliano photography provided by Tenute Tomasella.

The central part of the building is as much a work of art as are the wines; fundamentals of the winery dates back to the 16th century with a beautiful observation tower. This is not your ordinary winery--hand crated quality in every way.

I F A W I N E W E R E M E . . .

The limited production of bottles yearly include *award winning* white and red wines; they are most intriguing, rooted in high quality, interesting, pleasant and exquisitely unadulterated wines.

Additional information on the winery is available at http://www.tenute-tomasella.it/en/vini_fermi.php.

I F   A   W I N E   W E R E   M E . . .
WHICH WOULD IT BE?

GARGANEGA - (MOST REFER TO AS SOAVE - REGION WHERE IT IS PRIMARILY GROWN)

CHARACTERISTICS (ATTRIBUTES)	EXPRESSION (PERSONALITIES)	WINE STYLE (STYLE)	FINISH (DEMEANOR)
I am a neutral variety and much like a clean canvas when it comes to fruit, but I have nice white floral aromas, good minerality and solid crisp acidity. My body is usually slender to medium.	My personality remains calm and anchored without too much drama; I like to sport my natural floral aromas for a good time balancing with the subtle structure of my natural stone-like demeanor and comfortable attitude (acids). I am a nice sip!	Being from the northeastern Italy, I am steeped in a volcanic environment and often showcase my minerality in style, solid acids and pleasant white pedals of camomile. You'd like my style if you are less about fruit and more about my acids and pronounced floral quality.	I'm a good neutral conversation with hints of excitement from my acids. I can stand a clear point of view when it comes to my floral notes because I love sprinkling my natural touches on things around me. If you can handle a conversation comfortably, you'll appreciate me.

Place of origin, Veneto, Italy and has its roots in being dominantly a neutral variety. It is generally used as a dry wine with dominant notes of white flowers, slight minerality from the volcanic soils and substantial acidity. light to med body.

Food Styles of **Interest**: Anything works with this versatile varietal. Assuming that you have chosen wine from this varietal, identify a lighter protein food and/or mildly seasoned dishes to match this lighter floral varietal. Basic concepts to matching: wine acidity should exceed the food's acidity; wines residual sweetness should exceed the foods' sweetness; and the weight of the food should match that of the wine. Consider light meats and/or seafood; vegetable casseroles with a potato or cream base; and soft cheeses.

I F   A   W I N E   W E R E   M E . . .

GEWÜRZTRAMINER

CHARACTERISTICS (ATTRIBUTES)	EXPRESSION (PERSONALITIES)	WINE STYLE (STYLE)	FINISH (DEMEANOR)
I am a bit unique in that I have a natural lovely golden tint due to my pink skin; I tend to stand out with my unusual spice notes and complex aromas; I am most always full body but can be medium.	My personality reflects my style directly and is usually dry or medium-dry. My scents are of lovely tropical lychee (similar to a ripened pear) fruits, floral of fruit blossoms and dark flowers, a bit of spice with a smooth oil-like texture. My attitude (acids) are in check as they stay low to moderate. My demeanor is surprisingly unique.	My style allows me to explode with vast flavors in your mouth from my unique spice and tropical fruits, subtle floral notes that keeps the palate excited with a creamy texture. Try my sweet style as you may pick up fig and dried apricot notes... pure bliss.	I am one delicious surprise as many don't know what to expect when trying me out. I tend to excite your tongue with my spice, inviting fruit and waxy coating embrace; my finish provides a comfortable memorable engagement. Enjoy.

Place of origin, Alsace, France however the grape is grown in other regions with similar cool climates like Northern Italy, Northern Central Valley of CA, and Coastal parts of Chile and produces a range of styles (late harvest or sweet to dry). The grape is pink grape showcasing a wine of rich golden color, highly aromatic of orange blossoms, distinctive spice, lovely exotic fruit notes; moderate acid and substantial mouthfeel (oil coating); medium to fuller body wine. The balance of fruits and acidity remains straight through to the finish with its notable spice.

Food Styles of **Interest**: Anything works with this versatile varietal. Assuming that you have chosen wine from this varietal, identify a medium to heavy protein food and/or flavorful dishes to match this floral full body varietal. Basic concepts to matching: wine acidity should exceed the food's acidity; wines residual sweetness should exceed the foods' sweetness; and the weight of the food should match that of the wine. This varietal is great for most spice-driven Asian dishes (particularly Thai and Indian); pork and game; eggplant parmesan; and rich, fatty dishes and creamier soft cheeses.

I F   A   W I N E   W E R E   M E . . .
WHICH WOULD IT BE?

GRÜNER VELTLINER

CHARACTERISTICS (ATTRIBUTES)	EXPRESSION (PERSONALITIES)	WINE STYLE (STYLE)	FINISH (DEMEANOR)
I am somewhat of an enigma of the varieties as my flavor range morphs greatly thru maturation (and I am age-worthy). I am comfortable in my skins adding intensity and body. I'm generally light but can be medium body.	My personality can be quite diverse as my aromas and flavors start out crisp of fruit, slight stone-like, with a hint of spice which transforms into great complexity of minerality and fruity maturity And if I'm accessorized with oak, lovely depth surfaces.	My style can start out to the point of crisp green apples, slight minerals, with a hint of white pepper and then bam, evolve into great complexity of minerality and honey sweetness. Aging me in oak, I will deliver more complex layers of stoney minerals, concentrated fruit with slight pepper.	I am pleasant of crisp apples, pear and some minerals in my youth, with a subtle pepper finish; as I mature, you will see more integration of my minerals and concentrated fruit notes, maintaining pepper on the extended finish. Can create simple to complex memories, you decide.

Place of origin, lower Austria (Wachau) where the variety ripens well in the long growing season that it prefers. The flavors are most concentrated with a nice minerality and fruits; This wine has a wide range of maturation; it can be light or medium in body; flavors ranging from green apples and pear with some pepper on the finish to complex and intense of ripened apples, pear, pronounced minerals and slight pepper on the finish.

Food Styles of **Interest**: Pleasant and thought provoking food would be comfortable with wine from this varietal of subtle complexity. With this wine, identify a light protein food and/or mildly seasoned dishes to match this lighter floral varietal. Basic concepts to matching: wine acidity should exceed the food's acidity; the wine's residual sweetness should exceed the food's sweetness; the weight of the food should match that of the wine. Considerations include seafood with pasta and an herbal cream sauce; fishcakes; lamb or meat stew; vegetable pot-pie, whether cheese- or potato-based; and soft flavorful cheeses.

IF A WINE WERE ME . . .

WHICH WOULD IT BE?

MUSCADELLE - (NOT TO BE CONFUSED WITH MUSCAT OR MUSCADET)

CHARACTERISTICS (ATTRIBUTES)	EXPRESSION (PERSONALITIES)	WINE STYLE (STYLE)	FINISH (DEMEANOR)
I am the rare answer to what do you smell? Grapes, no truly accompanied with nice perfume accents. Given that my profile is distinctly grape, very little of me is needed to partner with other for either dry or sweet wines. Light to medium in body.	My personality can be a bit obvious with my expressive acids and perfumey and grapey nose but pleasant as my friends are always the more dominant cast. Sometimes, I can feel a bit conservative but show me some attention which helps build up my ego.	My style is always hanging with others as they bring out the best in me by rounding out my perfume-like taste. I am heard even when I whisper so I try to keep my sweetness and vibrant acids under wraps. I am always included in the fun as I help make it enjoyable. Look for my friends semillon and sauvignon blanc and you will find me.	If you appreciate a nice blend of aromatics, you will appreciate me and my friends. I love being with others and my conversation reflects this as I keep things pleasant, exciting and fashionably interesting.

Place of origin, Bordeaux, France. This is an aromatic variety with the quintessential grapey smell with lovely perfume notes. It is only used as a blend and in small proportions for both dry and sweet wines. This is a light to medium body wine which finishes with acidity and pleasant perfume notes.

Food Styles of Interest: Nice, light and easygoing food sits well with this inviting varietal. Assuming that you've chosen wine from this varietal, identify a light protein food and/or mildly seasoned dishes to match this lighter floral varietal. Basic concepts to matching: wine acidity should exceed the food's acidity; the wine's residual sweetness should exceed the food's sweetness; and the weight of the food should match that of the wine. Considerations include seafood, pasta and vegetables in a cream sauce; rice dishes with a cream/mushroom sauce; vegetable casseroles; and aged cheeses.

IF A WINE WERE ME . . .
WHICH WOULD IT BE?

PINOT GRIS / PINOT GRIGIO

CHARACTERISTICS (ATTRIBUTES)	EXPRESSION (PERSONALITIES)	WINE STYLE (STYLE)	FINISH (DEMEANOR)
I am clearly an individual, My natural moderate acidity and pleasant fruit notes allow me to be a pleasant drink all by my-self I have a wide range from light to full body, depends on where I'm grown. I'm in my prime in my youth, forever young!	My Alsatian roots shows my bolder personality of tropical fruit aromas, slight zest with a rich tex-ture and medium weight; Italian-wise, my personal-ity is more chill preferring to highlight my pro-nounced acids and keep my fruit aromas to a minimum and light body.	I love to show of my range of styles...my mango and melon notes, with some acids adds to the complexity of my creamy texture and fuller body being in Alsace. When in Italy, I keep my body trim, crisp youthful with lime waiting to stimulate your palate.	In Alsace, I take on a fuller body with very memorable tropical fruit taste that lingers a bit at-taching to my velvety texture...very pleasing. My Italian style is nice, quick and to the point, enjoying every simple sip...never complex.

Place of origin for **Pinot Gris** is Alsace, France. This expression is fuller body, with a creamy texture, tropical fruits of key lime and lemon curd, hints of spice and (often) a hint of residual sugar on the finish; and similar styles grown in many regions around the world notably Oregon (a much lighter style with apricot and often melon notes) Australia and New Zealand.

Place of origin for **Pinot Grigio** is Trentino, Italy producing a lighter more zesty style with crisp acid on the finish; similar style of wines in Oregon and Germany.

Food Styles of **Interest**: You'll need confident company with substantial conversation to keep up with the crispness of the wine from this varietal. If you have chosen this wine, identify a light protein food and/or mildly seasoned dishes to match this lighter floral varietal. Basic concepts to matching: wine acidity should exceed the food's acidity; the wine's residual sweetness should exceed the food's sweetness; and the weight of the food should match that of the wine. Italian style food would work well. Try a nice garden salad topped with a light meat, such as baked chicken or smoked whitefish and topped and crumbled with cheese to break down the acidity from the wine. Flavorful brined cheese and water crackers are another good option.

IF A WINE WERE ME...
WHICH WOULD IT BE?

RIBOLLA GIALLA

CHARACTERISTICS (ATTRIBUTES)	EXPRESSION (PERSONALITIES)	WINE STYLE (STYLE)	FINISH (DEMEANOR)
I am quite noticeable starting with my persistent vocal acids, floral bouquet, and often deep straw color. For sure, I am a solo player, but I can make pleasantry happen as a blend with others. I can seem boisterous for a white varietal, deceptively delicate and of a solid medium body giving to a great mouthfeel; however, I am a refreshing, yet substantive, sip of spicy amazement.	I can seem quite loud with my enthusiastic and energetic display of vibrant apple and peach acidity, inviting white floral scents, and sometimes an intriguing spicy finish. My medium body makes me a comfortable drink to be appreciated young or aged based on how I am vinified. People are attracted to my refreshing yet grounded perspective. Little is known about me outside of a few countries which keeps the wonder and mystique about me most enjoyable.	You can find me vinified dry (aged in oak or pure and lighter in stainless steel) or vividly in a sparkling style. All styles will show off my white floral aromatics and enthusiastic acids of lemon and fresh mouth-watering peach. I possess a hint of minerality and persistent spice on the finish, creating a sizzling attitude. No doubt, I stand out and I'm noticeable even when blended with other varietal friends like Friulano.	I am a poised, prominent figure and irresistible. Most people find me noticeably unique and intoxicating as I'm vocal with substance, which keeps the conversation going on for a long, saucy finish. I don't back away from sharing my perspective and I'm quite charming to listen to...get ready for a weighty discussion and lengthy greatness.

Place of origin is Greece but popularized in Friuli, Italy. This is a lovely aromatic variety vinified as a dry or sparkling style wine. Vivid vibrance of fresh peach and Granny Smith apple, providing hints of delicate flowers and spice, traced with stony qualities on the palate with a medium body. The finish is prominent with bright fresh peaches and lemon citrus, a slight almond paste, and highlighted with a hint of grapefruit peel and clove-like spice.

I F   A   W I N E   W E R E   M E . . .
WHICH WOULD IT BE?

Food Styles of **Interest**: Company in search of an explosively good time, afternoon or evening, would benefit from the vivaciousness of wine from this varietal. For this wine, identify a medium protein food and/or moderately seasoned dishes to match this vibrant, substantial and subtly spicy varietal. Basic concepts to matching: wine acidity should exceed the food's acidity, the wine's residual sweetness should exceed the food's sweetness and the weight of the food should match that of the wine. Consider meals with smoked fish, shellfish or seafood cooked in a light or medium cream sauce, sushi, fried food dishes, pasta and vegetables in a creamy sauce semi-soft and hard cheese, and hard breads.

I F A W I N E W E R E M E . . .
WHICH WOULD IT BE?

WHITE VARIETAL FEATURE - RIBOLLA GIALLA / LIVON, RONCALTO

Why RIBOLLA GIALLA? Most haven't even heard of the varietal and even less have tasted it, but you are in for a treat with this bold yet elegant white wine from **Livon.** Tenuta RoncAlto, the smallest of the Livon properties, is all about varietal representational experiences, exemplary quality, and more...this wine is quite statuesque with a solid foundation, the color is a medium straw, and the nose tantalizes with white fragrant flowers. It has the vibrance of fresh peaches and Granny Smith apple -- the palate is abundant of lively acidity yet deceptive with its undetected nuances - there is a subtle attitude of spice culminating this crisp yet luscious mouthfeel.

The finish of spice and vibrancy resonates for a nice long while. Ribolla Gialla from Livon is **strikingly beautiful from nose to tongue**!

I F   A   W I N E   W E R E   M E . . .

About **Livon and Tenuta RoncAlto** Vineyard...

The winery Livon was founded in 1964 with plots of land in the heart of Collio Friulano (Tenuta RoncAlto vineyards are there) and has since acquired additional farms. They not only produce stellar wine - olive oil and distillates are also made on their farms. The vineyards are spectacular to experience as is the Livon family running the properties. Family is at the core of it all...with their impeccable attention to detail, varietals are expressed exquisitely, and genuine charm and passion exudes from the family members straight into the bottle...a wonderment of *aesthetics and character.*

I F   A   W I N E   W E R E   M E . . .

WHICH WOULD IT BE?

The *RoncAlto Vineyard* produces Ribolla that is **beautifully prominent** with its energetic acids, fruits, and solid structural texture melded with a spiciness to produce a wine for the most engaging occasions. It's a pleasant yet bold indulgence in every sip.

Explore more about Livon: http://www.livon.it/   OR   http://www.livon.it/club.htm

IF A WINE WERE ME . . .

WHICH WOULD IT BE?

RIESLING

CHARACTERISTICS (ATTRIBUTES)	EXPRESSION (PERSONALITIES)	WINE STYLE (STYLE)	FINISH (DEMEANOR)
Naturally gifted with pleasant yet complex aromas...you should know that I pride myself on being pure yet powerful! I am a hardy variety and love to show off my natural array of aromas for you to decipher. I'm medium to full body with plenty of stamina.	My personality can vary based on how I'm brought up with my intense demeanor which you will grow to appreciate: I am versatile: dry (with my floral and fruit aromas; off-dry (with some sweetness on the palate); or sweet (still maintaining a bit of a spark from my natural acids).	From the Mosel, I can have a crazy complex style with mandarine oranges, apples and white peaches, a good bit of stoney minerality; or my Alsatian vines provides a fresh pine nose, slight petrol layered through pears, apples and baking spice--crazy intensity and more dry in style.	I am complex to decipher on the nose with all my intricacies but delicate on your palate with a surprisingly spicy linger. I know that I'm a sweet investment...I am designed to age well and maintain my complexity of acid and fruit sweetness. Discover me!

Place of origin, Mosel, Germany and widely planted around the world. The grape is a highly aromatic variety grown in different climates reflecting different flavors and styles. Rieslings retain their high levels of acidity no matter how they are vinified and can have nice floral and apple fruit notes from a cooler climate like Germany to a sweeter peach and citrus notes with a hint of pepper from warmer climates like Austria. Given the highly aromatic nature of this grape, it does not benefit from oak vessels as it needs an anaerobic environment to ferment as it retains its aromas. No matter where they are grown, the aromatics and fruit remain true to the end along with the prominent acids on the finish.

Food Styles of **Interest**: You'll appreciate company of deep intellect and good conversation to keep up with the complex subtleties and excitement of wine from this varietal. If you have chosen this wine, identify a medium protein food and/or moderately seasoned dishes to match this medium to full aromatic varietal. Basic concepts to matching: wine acidity should exceed the food's acidity; the wine's residual sweetness should exceed the food's sweetness; and the weight of the food should match that of the wine. German and some Italian style food would work well. Try a nice garden salad topped with a medium meat, such as baked chicken or smoked whitefish and topped and crumbled with cheese to break down the acidity from the wine. Flavorful brined cheese and water crackers are another good option.

I F   A   W I N E   W E R E   M E . . .

WHICH WOULD IT BE?

WHITE VARIETAL FEATURE - RIESLING / EFESTĒ

Why RIESLING? It is a beautiful varietal with an amazing nose, a complexity of flavors and an array of styles (dry to sweet). The grape color alone is wildly yellow green as a white variety, which is sure to capture interest. This particular wine by EFESTE is a lovely luscious **sip of approachable complexity** with delicate white peaches and mandarin oranges folded in nicely, excitable citrus fruit and a medium-full body.

...Why not! For one, Washington State wines are a necessity for wine appreciators and two, the EFESTĒ Winery utilizes natural yeast within the grapes creating flavors unique to each particular vineyard. You can't get more naturally character-driven than this as these wines have **pure personality!** The Evergreen Riesling will awaken your senses from its beautiful golden tinted yellow color to its honeysuckle flowers with yummy fruits on the nose.

IF A WINE WERE ME . . .
WHICH WOULD IT BE?

Its balanced vibrant acids and subtle sweetness of key limes, white peaches and apricots, plus hints of minerality luxuriating on the palate, provide, in a word, **splendor.** EFESTĒ Winery (pronounced "F-S-T" is an acronym for the winery's founders) is located throughout some of the best sites in the state of Washington, namely Columbia Valley and Yakima Valley. Their vineyard sites are laden with calcium richness from these ancient soils; so when it comes to taste of the terroir, this family has mastered it!

I F   A   W I N E   W E R E   M E . . .

Once you taste the character of these wines, their shared passion for **finely crafted wine** and the **art** of vinification is *evident*.

http://www.efeste.com

IF A WINE WERE ME . . .

WHICH WOULD IT BE?

SAUVIGNON BLANC/ FUME BLANC

CHARACTERISTICS (ATTRIBUTES)	EXPRESSION (PERSONALITIES)	WINE STYLE (STYLE)	FINISH (DEMEANOR)
I am most often accused of being outspoken with my vivid acids, varying fruits and a bit of green (grass-like quality). My fruit profile varies, generally you can expect green apples. My light body doesn't accept too much weighing me down. I'm a perfect drink in my youth.	I am worldly and very adaptable as I can display different profiles of vibrant fruits, apples, (often passion fruit); scents of green grass, herbs, and savory (vegetal)...I always show a happy, bright and youthful personality. Forever zesty.	My style is generally straight forward with citrus taste of lemons and limes almost always reveal me; my other qualities like green apples, (passionfruit), herbs and green bell pepper, help to create greater interest in me. When I am aged in oak, I pick up baking spice notes and even put on a bit of weight creating a medium body.	I start out the same way I finish, rather excitable with my acids, citrus, apples and often spice can linger for a little so the conversation is never dull. I tend to get a bit more complex and more rounded when aged in oak as my North American roots like to do with me. I'm quite versatile and easy to get along with if you can handle my POV on acids.

Place of origin, Loire Valley, France; however this is a widely planted grape across all of France and the world. This variety, generally is a light body with bright crisp acidity, can have a green/grass-like element; herbaceous quality, sometimes bell pepper along with passion fruit flavors, and finish with vibrancy of acidity.

In some regions like the U.S. where the grape is called Fume Blanc and often aged in oak creates slight complexity with a medium body, youthful and finishes with it's known acids.

Food Styles of **Interest**: Whether you have gregarious company (similar to this wine) or more subdued for a pleasant contrast, the varietal is quite vibrant. With a wine from this varietal, identify a light protein food and/or mildly seasoned dishes to match this lighter floral varietal. Basic concepts to matching: wine acidity should exceed the food's acidity; the wine's residual sweetness should exceed the food's sweetness; and the weight of the food should match that of the wine. Consider seafood and poultry - not too flavorful, but fat enough to hold up to the acids, and soft cheeses and light crackers.

SEMILLON

CHARACTERISTICS (ATTRIBUTES)	EXPRESSION (PERSONALITIES)	WINE STYLE (STYLE)	FINISH (DEMEANOR)
I am widely known in my region of Bordeaux with vast uses but illness-prone due to my thin skin. I am the rich texture of dried fruits when used in a blend with S. Blanc and Muscadelle for sweet styles; and provide the body and acids for complexity in dry blends. Medium-full body and age well. In Australia, I hang solo with my range varying from light and crisp to full and complex body.	My personality is outgoing and you can count on me being with others. I'm generally the life of the party with my gregarious attitude (acids) and nice structured body I provide complexity with my balance of sweetness and acidity to most of my blended sweet friends. When rolling solo, I can come across energetic and bubbly or complex and intriguing.	My style back home in Bordeaux is to hang with my other varieties helping to make an awesome taste, whether sweet or dry blends. You are guaranteed to taste my acids and sweet texture from noble rot or my solid bones when dry. In Australia, you decide which style suits you best as I vary from light and crisp of green apples to medium body of toast and honey when allowed to age.	1 can be as simple or complex as you'd like based on the style you prefer. If you want straight forward and substantial, that's me; if you want complexity and dialogue, that's me; or if you want energetic, youth with some attitude still, that's me. I'm everything you can want, just be prepared.

Place of origin, Bordeaux, France where it is a thin skinned variety prone to noble rot and notably used for fuller body sweet wines. This is a variety that ages well and provides both richness of color and texture. It is generally blended with Sauvignon Blanc and Muscadelle for the beautiful sweet wines of Sauternes. Semillon provides an opulent texture, with acidity and sweetness on the finish.

Also important region for Semillon is HunterValley, Australia where it is usually vinified as a single variety; a lighter style with crisp acids but capable of picking up more complexity of flavors with age. In other parts of Australia, the herbaceous quality can get a bit confusing for many. The body and finish will vary here based on where it is produced in Australia from crisp and light body to complex with honey and toast, and full in body.

Food Styles of **Interest**: Company of any kind works well with this drink, but easy going may be best with the energized wine from this varietal . When choosing this wine, identify a medium protein food and/or moderately flavored dish to match this vibrancy of this varietal. Basic concepts to matching: wine acidity should exceed the food's acidity (this is an acidic wine); the wine's residual sweetness should exceed the food's sweetness; and the weight of the food should match that of the wine. Heavier creamier dishes will help break up the acidity. Also, select medium meats of seafood, like game or tuna, vegetable and herb casseroles and softer cheeses.

TORRONTES

CHARACTERISTICS (ATTRIBUTES)	EXPRESSION (PERSONALITIES)	WINE STYLE (STYLE)	FINISH (DEMEANOR)
I'm an aromatic variety of bold fruit notes accented with a pleasant floral fragrance; balanced acid and medium body. I am generally solo and make lovely company for anytime of day or night.	My personality can come across as overwhelming with my fragrant fruit and perfumed flowers but balanced with a tamed attitude (acids). I allow all aspects of me to be vocal so this may seem confident but I believe you will like the experience.	I am sincerely a lovely taste as I shower your palate with all of my peach, apricot and apple flavors, adorned with my soft white floral perfume. I can be pleasantly surprising as my acids are just as comfortable expressing my POV.	If you can appreciate some complexity, you and I will be just fine as I speak in subtleties. Just a little patience and my platform for discussion will linger nicely with interest of acids and natural sugars. Try me!

Place of origin, still being determined but most dominantly grown in Salta Province, Argentina. This is an aromatic variety usually vinified dry. Exudes delicious flavors of ripe peach, honeydew, pear; accented with tropical bouquet of flowers; and crisp acidity. Most are medium bodied wines with a lengthy finish of balanced acids and tropical fruits.

I F   A   W I N E   W E R E   M E . . .

Food Styles of **Interest**: Company is not needed, but always appreciated with a balanced excitable varietal like this one. Assuming that you have chosen wine from this varietal, identify a light protein food and/or mildly seasoned dishes to match this lighter floral varietal. Basic concepts to matching: wine acidity should exceed the food's acidity; the wine's residual sweetness should exceed the food's sweetness; and the weight of the food should match that of the wine. Consider tapas veggie or seafood; cerviche; seafood and rice; chicken tacos; and rice and herbal vegetable casseroles.

WHICH WOULD IT BE?

VIOGNIER

CHARACTERISTICS (ATTRIBUTES)	EXPRESSION (PERSONALITIES)	WINE STYLE (STYLE)	FINISH (DEMEANOR)
I am an aromatic variety of pleasant fruit and floral notes, slight minerality and a velvety texture. My body varies from medium to full based on where I'm grown. Warmer climates are best for me..just have to watch my sugars weight as I become less interesting.	My personality appears delicate with pleasant aromas of tropical fruits and flowers but once you get to know me you will see there is depth with my rich texture and moderate acids. I am easy to get to know but can get boozy. I am medium to full body that handles oak cautiously.	My style is generally beautiful dry or off-dry, my exotic fruit aromas of pear, apricot with slight clove adds such accents. I am usually balanced as my acids don't get too out of hand but my sugars can--creating a bit more alcohol/attitude to surface. I can hold up to most any competition.	I have been told that I'm harmonious to drink, I have a tendency to get boastful with alcohol based on my natural sugars...be forewarned. I have a natural baking spice finish that lingers with my lovely apricot, pear fruit and white floral notes of honeysuckle. Nice conversation piece.

Place of origin, Rhone Valley, France and growing popularity in California, Virginia and Australia. This is a beautiful aromatic variety vinified dry. Nicely balanced with succulent pear and apricot, a nice waxy texture, and medium to full body. The finish is polished with a pleasing layering of clove in with the fruit and slight acidity of lime.

Food Styles of **Interest**: Company celebrating an elegant occasion would be ideal with wine from this varietal. For this wine, identify a medium protein food and/or moderately seasoned dishes to match this aromatic velvety varietal. Basic concepts to matching: wine acidity should exceed the food's acidity; the wine's residual sweetness should exceed the food's sweetness; and the weight of the food should match that of the wine. Consider meals with shellfish or seafood cooked in a medium sauce of cream or oil; roasted chicken and vegetables; medium meats, slightly spicy Thai dishes; smoked fish; and rice casseroles or veggie and/or chicken pot pies in a potato base.

WHITE VARIETAL FEATURE - VIOGNIER / CINDER

Why VIOGNIER? No brainer...not very known but a spectacular drink experience to have. I want to be the first perhaps, to introduce you to a http://cinderwines.com/dry-viognier/, white fresh flowers with pear and peach notes on the nose, luscious mouthfeel of peach, pear and tangerine peel folds in nicely with nice vibrancy of crisp acids and medium body.

...Why not!

Boise, Idaho, seriously! Well many people wouldn't have even considered Boise on the map of wines ...look out as **Cinder** has a different story to share and inform with this **gorgeous consistent sip of elegance**.

Their Viognier in any style is quite exquisite. A **balanced yet powerful** composition of flavors that float on your palate with a pleasant continuous creamy yet crisp finish of limes, peaches, and slight stoney minerality.

A little info about the winery...

Cinder is located in Snake River Valley, Idaho and it is abundant in geology of varying soils. The Dry Viognier is a continuation of their love affair with Snake River Valley Viognier grape as they strive to show the depth of character and versatility of this variety in their region, so they make several styles.

The Winemaker... **Melanie Krause**, grew up in Boise, Idaho where she spent much of her time in her family's huge garden which included a collection of 40+ varieties of grapes! She attended Washington State University worked in wheat genetics and breeding, graduated with bachelor degrees in Biology and Spanish. Worked as a vineyard technician and gained invaluable skills under knowledgeable viticulturists. Melanie began working for Chateau Ste Michelle and studied under three great winemakers, Bob Bertheau, Ron Bunnell and Kendall Mix. Now she and her husband Joe Schnerr are the owners of their own winery, Cinder Winery.

http://cinderwines.com/index.htm

WINE SPEAK - RED

RED / BLACK GRAPE VARIETIES

Before we expand upon the characteristics of the red varieties, you should know more about their growth process and how they are made into wines. Making red wine can be considered even closer to an art and a science than producing white wines with regards to obtaining just the right balance of flavors and texture during fermentation based on the desired result.

VINIFICATION

The process for making red wines can be a lot more involved given the fermentation on their skins extracting tannins along with color. During fermentation, red wines are in *constant* contact with their skins (oftentimes seeds/pips and stems are included) from which they derive their colors, complex flavors and character, including tannins. The winemaker has decisions to make when it comes to how much extraction and how long to macerate the juice on the skins, adjustments to temperature during fermentation, determination of techniques for tannin and/or color control, and almost always malolactic fermentations (conversion of tart malic acids into smoother, creamy lactic acids).

So think about this for a moment when you are tasting. Notice what is often referred to as structure and texture, as your palate is heavily influenced by the effect of tannins from the skin and/or oak when aged in oak vats; this is where the artistic **balance and/or style preference** of the winemaker is at play.

Cabernet Franc Grape

Cabernet Franc bottled

Cabernet Franc pour

I F   A   W I N E   W E R E   M E . . .

VITICULTURE

The caretaker responsibilities are the same for red wines as for whites; however, extra care has to be taken to ensure the sugars and tannins of the grapes are properly ripened before picking. If the sugars are not ripe enough, the result is less flavor and lower alcohol, and if the tannins are not ripe enough the result is harsher astringency to manipulate.

Merlot

Pinot Noir

Tempranillo

IF A WINE WERE ME . . .

WHICH WOULD IT BE?

AGLIANICO

CHARACTERISTICS (ATTRIBUTES)	EXPRESSION (PERSONALITIES)	WINE STYLE (STYLE)	FINISH (DEMEANOR)
I'm solo and known to very few, but gaining notice with my deep garnet color, powerful structure of sucking acids and firm tannins, layered with a medley of dark fruits. I am strong willed and require aging so patience is needed. I make for great conversation.	My personality can seem stately as I speak loud with my acidity and clear with a backbone. I have lots to say and when you allow me time to age (love oak on me). You will get all my complexities of dark cherries and berries, and a whiff of floral scent.	I'm very pronounced from beginning to end with flavors of rich, bold dark fruits, sucking acids and robust tannins in my youth. As I age, I mellow nicely, behaving as a dedicated partner of complexity with mature plums and chocolate sweetness.	I'm not one that you will likely forget, as I linger around long after the start in my youth and maturity. I am capable of hanging out until the wee hours talking it up because I can. How about you!

Place of origin is Campania, Italy by way of the Greeks. These deep brownish red wines can be quite aggressive, generally vinified dry, and tend to be full bodied with tighter tannins and vibrant acidity (helps the wine to age well). Aglianico wines are best matured for a few years as the acids mellow, allowing the fruit to become more prominent and the bold tannins better integrated.

Food Styles of **Interest**: Mellow company would contrast rather nicely with the rich bold flavors of wine from this varietal. When selecting this wine, identify a higher protein food and/or bold flavored dish to match this heavier structure of acids, tannins and dark fruity varietal. Basic concepts to matching: wine acidity should exceed the food's acidity; the wine's residual sweetness should exceed the food's sweetness; and the weight of the food should match that of the wine. Consider rich meats such as beef; heavier rich pasta dishes; and big aged cheeses - even cave-aged blue cheese with dried fruits would be lovely.

I F   A   W I N E   W E R E   M E . . .

BRUNELLO (DI MONTALCINO) - clone of SANGIOVESE

CHARACTERISTICS (ATTRIBUTES)	EXPRESSION (PERSONALITIES)	WINE STYLE (STYLE)	FINISH (DEMEANOR)
I am a unique clone of the Sangiovese family dedicated to the Montalcino region. I am solo, always made of superior structure, bold acidity - a rich dark fruit creating deep red hues, with hints of herbs and cocoa making me complete. Hold on to me as I age well and am a keeper...long live structured elegance!	My personality is confident with firm structure and well-rounded sophistication. I am a complete solo package, you will not likely see me blended. My aromas are of ripened dark cherries and raspberries, often with scents of saddlebags, plus dark chocolate and herbs.	My style is all about dry, bold structure, and I'm balanced with racy acids and dark raspberries, cherries and blackberries. I can be more fruit forward but still have a firm structure early on. With maturity, I'm a fine sip of something wonderfully complex with my ripened fruits, dust, subtle spice and cocoa.	I am poised; although my confidence can be straightforward, it includes elegance and stimulation. Not likely forgotten! I am never too demanding, so have a sip and see that I am one balanced glass of finesse....enjoy!

Place of origin is Montalcino, Tuscany. Brunello is a specific clone of the Sangiovese grape which must be vinified 100% as a single varietal (no blend of other varietals) in Montalcino, whereby Sangiovese used for Chianti can include a blend of other grape varietals. This wine requires aging for a few years and can age for decades, due in part to its lively acids, round tannins, and pronounced dark fruits with hints of cocoa.

Food Styles of **Interest**: This would be great company that you want to shower with the finer tastes... Assuming that you have chosen wine from this varietal, identify a medium to heavy protein food and/or flavorful dishes to match this medium to full varietal. Basic concepts to matching: wine acidity should exceed the food's acidity; the wine's residual sweetness should exceed the food's sweetness; and the weight of the food should match that of the wine. Food considerations: pasta and a cream/marinara sauce; roasted vegetables (portabella mushrooms) and pasta; portabella mushroom burger and cheese; and medium meats like lamb and venison.

I F   A   W I N E   W E R E   M E . . .

CABERNET FRANC

CHARACTERISTICS (ATTRIBUTES)	EXPRESSION (PERSONALITIES)	WINE STYLE (STYLE)	FINISH (DEMEANOR)
I'm known for my ability to blend well with others, namely helping mellow my offspring Cabernet Sauvignon and supporting my friend Merlot. Single, you can enjoy the elegance of softer tannins, medium body, slight spice, vegetal, floral perfume, and my pale red hues.	My personality is versatile, as I express myself with medium tension (tannins), moderate acids (vibrancy) of raspberry, lovely perfume aromatics of violets, vegetal earthiness and a hint of black pepper; Being even keel, I harmonize my bold and my subtle buds.	My style can vary based on where I'm grown. When solo and made dry I'm decked out in sweet dark floral notes, earthy vegetal quality, fit and charming. When hanging with others, I can be the anchor to lean on or the touch of elegance to round them out. I am known for my diversity.	I am adaptable and make for nice conversation. I am a good listener yet can hold on to my POV without overwhelming the discussion/finish. You can expect great versatility and good times with me.

Place of origin, Bordeaux, France. This variety is vinified as in important component in Bordeaux blend and as a high performing single varietal in Tourraine in the Loire Valley of France. Wines produced from Cabernet Franc will maintain structure, distinctive vegetal notes, pleasant dark red fruits, hints of pepper spice with a floral scent. They can range from med to full bodied with integrated tannins and medium acidity, and will age for several years.

Food Styles of **Interest**: You will need some charming and enjoyable buds. For wine from this varietal, identify a medium protein food and/or moderately seasoned dish to match the structure and enhance the floral aspects and harmonize the earthiness of this varietal. Basic concepts to matching: wine acidity should exceed the food's acidity; the wine's residual sweetness should exceed the food's sweetness; and the weight of the food should match that of the wine. Food considerations include root vegetable casserole, roasted lamb and herbs with sweet tender vegetables.

I F   A   W I N E   W E R E   M E . . .

RED VARIETAL FEATURE - CABERNET FRANC / BARBOURSVILLE

Why CABERNET FRANC?

This varietal is super interesting and not enough people have really tasted this varietal expressed as a true Cabernet Franc...do yourself a favor and check it out. If you can't make it to Tourraine in Loire Valley France, this wine will make for a lovely substitute. You are sure to experience a **palate of harmonious complexity** filled with fine memories that stick around for a bit--a stellar representation from Barboursville in VA.

...Why not!

Perhaps for fear of drooling...no seriously, this Barboursville Cabernet Franc is extraordinaire with full intention to satisfy with its **luscious** ripened fruit **berries** layered in with plums and dried figs; the acids and **welcoming** tannins continue to hum **balanced** throughout with a bit of mushroom earthiness on the lengthy finish.

I F   A   W I N E   W E R E   M E . . .

WHICH WOULD IT BE?

A little info about the winery...

Barboursville Vineyards, in Barboursville, VA, has already made its thumbprint known; their disciplined talent has led to establishing the credibility of the Virginia appellation, cultivating wines of a European heritage which wholly justify this new terroir. Barboursville is committed to grape cultivation and in crafting wines of inherent food-friendliness.

All Cabernet Franc photography courtesy of Barboursville Vineyards

The *Winemaker* **Luca Paschina** was born into a winemaking family in Piemonte, Italy, where he also took his degree in oenology from Umberto I Academy. He has been winemaker at Barboursville Vineyards since 1991. His vintages of Cabernet Franc led to international recognition of the varietal in Virginia, with the Governor's Cup award for his 1997 vintage and numerous Gold Medals and other honors thereafter from wine competitions and critics throughout the nation and in the United Kingdom. Need I say more... locate their amazing wines at:
http://www.barboursvillecellar.com

IF A WINE WERE ME . . .

WHICH WOULD IT BE?

CABERNET SAUVIGNON

CHARACTERISTICS (ATTRIBUTES)	EXPRESSION (PERSONALITIES)	WINE STYLE (STYLE)	FINISH (DEMEANOR)
I am a very popular variety with roots all over the world. I exude a lot of confidence with my natural bold structure (which LOVES oak). Nice acidity, mint and fruit notes make me distinguishable, along with my dark garnet color. If you don't have the patience for me to age, check me out as a blend with my parent Cab Franc, which softens my structure while I back up my friends like Merlot, Malbec, etc. We are well known in Bordeaux (crowned blend).	I am gregarious and love to hang out...I'm a bit boastful just to remind you of my natural talents! I am usually the dominant one among the friends that I normally blend with because of my amazing full body, beautiful dark plum and currant fruits, hints of cassis and chocolate for accent. When in oak, I mellow a tad bit...but I'm still quite bold. I am definitely more relaxed when hanging with others...and they love being with me.	My style is notably bold as a solo player. I stand out with my firm structure, vibrant acids and dark berries, with hints of menthol. In my maturity, I'm tempered a bit and in my native home of Bordeaux I'm usually **the** backbone of the blended team. In Cali, I am a daring individual, quite complex with dark concentrated fruits, herbs, mushrooms and do well with age. Mendoza shows me off with more jammy fruit notes, a medium body and smoother tannins.	No matter which place you've tasted me, my structure will be memorable. I make for a long conversation that lingers until the bitter end. I am less of a loose cannon in my maturity and make for nice dialogue. If you appreciate bold, confident... then it's good times with me. Enjoy, as most do!

Place of origin is Bordeaux France; however this varietal is one of the more commonly produced grapes grown around the world and has just as many distinct flavor characteristics based on the climates where grown. It is vinified as a dry wine of full body. Regardless of where it's grown, the grape is known to be consistently tannic due to its thick skins and combined with the high acidity and black currant fruit. The cooler the climate, the fruit can highlight the mint notes and exhibit more earth with age. The warmer weather will make for more stewed fruit profile and often vegetal, while mild climates maintain the fresher taste of berries. This is why you may notice a difference in the taste of a Cab Sauvignon from one region to the next (based on the climate and winemaker choices). Cab Sauvignon really benefits from being fermented in oak barrels - while contributing to its body, it helps to soften the tannins and increase distinct flavors. As a notable blend around the world (Bordeaux in France, Super Tuscan in Italy, and Meritage in the U.S.), its function in a blend can range from color and fruit to solid structure and age-ability.

Food Styles of **Interest**: Any and all kinds of company will do with wine from this varietal although it has such a hefty ego it doesn't really need any. Assuming you've chosen this wine, identify a heavier protein food and/or richly flavored dish to match the strength and tannic texture of this varietal. Basic concepts to matching: wine acidity should exceed the food's acidity; the wine's residual sweetness should exceed the food's sweetness; and the weight of the food should match that of the wine. This wine is obviously better suited for heavier meats as well as heavier seafood - tuna (grilled) can hold up to the tannins and highlight the fruit notes. Other options would be a typical old fashioned hamburger filled with herbs; pasta and herb rich marinara sauce; and seared tuna steaks with herbs.

IF A WINE WERE ME . . .
WHICH WOULD IT BE?

CARMENERE

CHARACTERISTICS (ATTRIBUTES)	EXPRESSION (PERSONALITIES)	WINE STYLE (STYLE)	FINISH (DEMEANOR)
I was readily adopted by my Chilean families - they encourage me to strut with spicy excitement. I am more of an individual, but can be seen blending with other varieties. My abundant dark fruit qualities stand out with natural spice giving interest to my medium structure. My hues are pleasantly dark blueish red.	My personality is clearly spicy yet versatile enough to mix well with others offering intrigue along with my cherry notes. I like to please - I provide excitement in my youth and am meant to be appreciated young.	I am pretty straight forward as a dry wine. This means I'm quite comfortable all by myself strutting my beautiful dark crimson color, seemingly bold with spice and cherry fruit notes, calm tannins and acidity. You will definitely notice me whether solo or hanging with others, or on my own as a single varietal.	If you can handle some flare and alluring playfulness in a conversation, you will enjoy hanging with me. I always have a catchy line or two to add. I stay on the surface and keep things exciting – don't worry, I will not get too complex. I'm always a great start with my spunky nature.

Place of origin is Bordeaux France, but abandoned and embraced as a prominent Chilean varietal. This is a moderately fragrant single varietal and known for its red pepper spiciness, dark red fruits, soft tannins and medium body. It is generally rich with dark red fruit, lighter acids and medium tannins and body. As a blend, it adds bold color and pepper spice notes.

Food Styles of **Interest**: Wine from this varietal would be best suited for chill company for contrast or more saucy fun company to meld. For this wine, identify a medium weight protein food and/or light to medium seasoned dishes so as not to overwhelm the fruitiness and lighter body of this varietal. Basic concepts to matching: wine acidity should exceed the food's acidity; the wine;s residual sweetness should exceed the food's sweetness; and the weight of the food should match that of the wine. Food considerations: tapas (meat or vegetables), rice casseroles, and nutty cheeses.

IF A WINE WERE ME . . .
WHICH WOULD IT BE?

CINSAULT

CHARACTERISTICS (ATTRIBUTES)	EXPRESSION (PERSONALITIES)	WINE STYLE (STYLE)	FINISH (DEMEANOR)
I am an ancient variety and not widely recognized outside of France. I LOVE blending with my friends and bringing out the best in them. I've been told that I fill a room with my amazing floral and fruit aromatics; I provide the finesse that my structured friends need-- softening their edgy tannins. I have a slim solid body and quite fruit luscious with my ruby hues.	My personality is definitely adaptable and outgoing with my pleasant bouquet of black and blue fruits, beautiful floral and perfume notes enhancing any occasion.	I am versatile with my fragrant way of being; as a single varietal, a blend, or even a Rosé. When you check me out hanging with my friends like Carignan, Syrah Grenache and/or Mourvedre, I *am* the pleasant one of the bunch! When solo, I am fruitlicious yet structured! I enjoy keeping the company entertained.	I tend to be very outgoing and friendly; love being with friends and supporting them when needed. I love light hearted conversations and won't overstay my welcome unless of course my friends are lingering on, then I get caught up with them. I offer a nice and substantial conversation...let's chat.

Place of origin is southern France. Cinsault is also *known* as **Hermitage** in South Africa and is one of the parents to the famed Pinotage clone (Pinot Noir + Hermitage). This is an ancient variety that is vinified dry and as a rosé; wines produced from Cinsault benefit from the grapes' inherent fruity, floral notes and lighter body with some rusticity. It makes for a nice simple yet solid every day sip or a pleasant blending component in a Rosé.

Food Styles of **Interest**: This is all about adventurous company and those seeking less known wines. Assuming that you have chosen wine from this varietal, identify a light to medium protein food and/or mildly seasoned dishes to match this lighter floral varietal. Basic concepts to matching: wine acidity should exceed the food's acidity; the wine's residual sweetness should exceed the food's sweetness; and weight of the food should match that of the wine. Food considerations include light seafood, poultry, or meat; herb-marinated vegetables and light rice; and soft to medium mild cheeses.

IF A WINE WERE ME . . .

WHICH WOULD IT BE?

GAMAY

CHARACTERISTICS (ATTRIBUTES)	EXPRESSION (PERSONALITIES)	WINE STYLE (STYLE)	FINISH (DEMEANOR)
I'm an upbeat single varietal; most known for my lighter outgoing fruity goodness, natural hyper acids, (usually tamed though) and accented with floral perfume, light to medium body and deep ruby hues. I am often mistaken for a light pinot noir, but I can be more complex based on the soils I'm planted in.	Fragrant w/fresh cherry, raspberry, dark flowers and lighter structure. Popular persona is Beaujolais Nouveau- super light and bubblegum scent. However, in the Cru sense (class of wine/ vines), I am more confident with a full body, velvety tannins, and balanced expression of vibrance and elegance. And age worthy.	As a simple Beaujolais Nouveau, I am light-hearted and ready to party with my flamboyant ways. As a Cru, I am quite sophisticated, have a strong POV about my structure yet have balanced energy and outlook with my acids and fruit I can be more complex and balanced based on where grown and how vinified.	People love having me around for light conversation when in my Nouveau state of being. However, that is far from my extent. I can hold the deepest of conversations and linger on in your mind once you explore me in the Cru sense. I'm a nice, complex yet balanced discussion...you only need to decide what works best.

Place of origin is Burgundy, France. Mostly known as Beaujolais and Beaujolais Nouveau (as a simpler style produced by carbonic maceration made specifically for the annual fabricated Holiday, the third Thursday of November). Carbonic maceration is a technique used to extract the rich color without the tannins and maintain the fresh fruit quality, but leaves a nose of candied fruit and bubble gum. Gamay is generally vinified dry as a single varietal, with a palate of fresh *or* ripe red and blueberries. Acids are generally vibrant but can be tempered, and the body can range from light to full.

Food Styles of **Interest**: All kinds of company will work with wine from this varietal. When choosing this wine, identify a lighter to medium protein food and/or moderate seasoned dish to enhance the structure, acidity and texture of this varietal. Basic concepts to matching: wine acidity should exceed the food's acidity; the wine's residual sweetness should exceed the food's sweetness; and the weight of the food should match that of the wine. Food considerations: grilled salmon and roasted meats for the Cru style, light poultry, lamb, baked vegetables or light cheeses for the Beuajolais style.

IF A WINE WERE ME . . .
WHICH WOULD IT BE?

GRENACHE/GARNACHA

CHARACTERISTICS (ATTRIBUTES)	EXPRESSION (PERSONALITIES)	WINE STYLE (STYLE)	FINISH (DEMEANOR)
I'm definitely a single varietal yet great company when blended. Basking in the sun with my thin skin, my fruit notes are more concentrated, with subtle spice, smooth tannins, high alcohol and pale ruby hues. In Spain, my intense dark fruits and super firm tannins showcase my complexity with deep ruby hues.	I can be quite versatile but the constant with me is red and black fruit fragrance, light tannic structure and a hidden pleasant subtle expression of spiciness. When I'm mixing with my friends, I am still prominent of fragrance and body because of my boozy (high alcohol) nature.	I can range from your easy everyday drink to your fine occasional wine from Priorat. I can display simplicity with a twist of fire or an elegance that entices you to want to take me along. When I'm fortified, my style is always sweet with a nice mouthfeel and full body (not to be surprised by my delicate color).	My conversation will range from simple to thought provoking. . It depends on what you are in the mood for. I am well rounded and capable of blending in most situations...I just need to know what style of me you are after. I'm here to satisfy with a nice subtle flame that can linger or end more abruptly.

Place of Origin is Rioja, Spain (and central) where it is known as Garnacha. Outside of Spain, the varietal is known as Grenache. Garnacha/Grenache is a widely popular planted grape around the world and vinified as dry wines, Rose, and Fortified. The common element of this diversely produced wine is the beautiful red and dark fruits, whether fresh and elegant or concentrated and bold; as well as its minimal tannic quality due to its thin skins. The body will range from med to full, based upon where it is grown and how it is vinified. The same can be said about the color and fruit concentration on the palate. Grenache is a popular blend in Rhone Valley, France, as is GSM in Australia along with Syrah and Mourvedre, or as a full body fortified wine in Australia or Vin Doux Naturel in southern France.

Food Styles of **Interest**: This is all about enjoyable company and those looking for a robust time. Assuming that you have chosen wine from this varietal, identify a medium protein food and/or moderately flavored dish to match the structure of this varietal (based on where it is vinified). Basic concepts to matching: wine acidity should exceed the food's acidity; the wine's residual sweetness should exceed the food's sweetness; and the weight of the food should match that of the wine. From Spain, this wine will pair nicely with stews, grilled meats to match the more tannic structure or game; and nice hard flavorful cheeses. **Other than** Spanish Garnacha or Rhone Valley France Grenache, try pasta dishes with lighter marinara or cream sauces, lighter meats like rabbit and nice, hard nutty cheeses.

MALBEC / AUXERROIS

CHARACTERISTICS (ATTRIBUTES)	EXPRESSION (PERSONALITIES)	WINE STYLE (STYLE)	FINISH (DEMEANOR)
I have historical roots south of Bordeaux with my inky skin, highly tannic, complex dark fruits and deep blue hues. I am adaptable as a blend in Bordeaux wines and as a single intense player. My single characteristics are appreciated in Argentina with a firm body of smooth tannins, and concentrated black fruits accented with spice.	I am as much an independent soul as I am about keeping people around. I don't mind showcasing my tannic, dark berry fruit qualities and sometimes enhanced floral notes. I blend well with others and you will always notice my support as I provide quite a bit of structure to keep my friends anchored.	My individual style is generally a dry wine. In Mendoza, Argentina I am elegantly confident with velvety smooth tannins, luscious dark fruit, full body and perfume-like (even as a Rosé). In Cahors, France I'm more outspoken with my boldly pronounced tannins, concentrated fruit berries and a bit of earthiness. Mixing with others (of Cahors and Bordeaux), my firm structure and fruit juiciness add attitude.	You should be secure enough to hang with me as an individual or with friends. I speak out comfortably, arguably I can be a bit forward, but still have a balanced approach. You should know that conversations are rarely light with me as I linger on for a while, increasing the complexity and topic. Take time with me as I'm worth it.

Place of Origin is southwest France (namely Cahors whereby Malbec is known as Auxerrois) and throughout different parts of the country. Malbec is most notably grown in Mendoza, Spain, and other regions in the U.S., Canada, and New Zealand. It is vinified as a dry wine of single varietal or a blend and as a Rosé; these are full body wines with dark floral, dark berry fruit notes and distinguished with their purple bluish hues (much like blue ink). And, as a blend, the full body structure of this varietal is maintained.

I F   A   W I N E   W E R E   M E . . .

Food Styles of **Interest**: This is company that can handle some tough conversation and likes to eat with their drink. Assuming that you have chosen wine from this varietal, identify a heavier protein food and/or richly flavored dish to match the body and tannic texture of this varietal. Basic concepts to matching: wine acidity (this is lower acidity) should exceed the food's acidity; the wines residual sweetness should exceed the food's sweetness; and the weight of the food should match that of the wine. Hardier foods like a steak or any grilled meats would be good examples of 'like' textures. Heavier casseroles, like lasagna, and flavorful hard cheeses would also be good pairings.

I F   A   W I N E   W E R E   M E . . .

RED VARIETAL FEATURE - MALBEC / FINCA DECERO

Why Malbec? Malbec is making a nice name for itself as a red varietal of interest and intrigue with its massive structure and delicate nose. And this isn't your ordinary aggressive Malbec; instead, it is a harmonized display of *tough guy meets delicate girl*. The depth of color is amazing – a blueish black, with a lovely bouquet of violets and fruits on the nose and the rich texture of ripened berries layered on top of a harmoniously firm structure. Hold on for a beautiful marriage of flavors on the palate with this Decero Malbec, truly **exquisite complexity!**

 ... **Why Not!** Decero Malbec is an elegant expression of Argentinian Malbec. This wine is a **stunning combination** of flavors on the palate with tamed tannins that are balanced with vibrant acidity. Dark ripe blackberries, blueberries, raspberries and red plums are nicely integrated with subtleties of vanilla spice and dried sweet flowers on the continuous finish.

WHICH WOULD IT BE?

Finca Decero is located in Argentina's Agrelo sub-appellation of Mendoza. Finca Decero is sensitive to the environment and to the natural attributes of the sustainably farmed Remolinos Vineyard. Malbec is one of their five *single vineyards* (single vineyard Malbec is rare in Argentina). Due to the precise attention to viticulture, these wines are very elegant with great violet aromatics that are prominent in Malbec from the single vineyard Remolinos.

Given its disciplined approach when producing wines, it is not surprising that Finca Decero was named in the 'T**op 10 Producers of Argentina**' by Decanter in 2011.

IF A WINE WERE ME . . .

WHICH WOULD IT BE?

MERLOT

CHARACTERISTICS (ATTRIBUTES)	EXPRESSION (PERSONALITIES)	WINE STYLE (STYLE)	FINISH (DEMEANOR)
My gift is versatility but I am most significant mingling with my friends, most notably one of the three blends in Bordeaux, and I can be a simple single varietal. You can find me sporting a nice array of black or red fruits based on my harvest, always soft tannins, and I am medium to full body with rich dark blueish hues. Easy going!	My personality is adaptable - when by myself my aromas are inviting of blueberries, blackberries, black plums and currants, soft tannins, low acid and a bit boozy (not complex, just chill). My velvety texture, pleasant fruits and boozy body brings out the best in my friends.	My style can vary as a single varietal from dark rich fruits, high alcohol and soft tannins to a medley of fresh red/black fruits, raspberries, higher acids and earthy notes. As a blend, my style brings out the elegance and depth in others. It's usually a chill time when indulging me - if not overly decked in oak!	I am well versed and easy to connect with; I don't create much intensity but keep the conversation afloat with interesting comments. I am a good anchor to my sometimes boastful friends as I'm about keeping everything even keel, but love making sure we have a good time. My approachable nature is memorable!

Place of origin is southwest France (namely Bordeaux) and throughout France. This grape varietal is usually vinified dry and mostly as a blend, but can fine as a single varietal. It is naturally deep colored, fruity, slight tannins yet boozy alcohol making it medium to full body. It is a key blend in the Bordeaux and likely is the most planted because its affinity to grow in diverse soils.

Food Styles of **Interest**: This is great, easygoing company with a lighter side of the discussion. Assuming that you've chosen wine from this varietal, identify a lighter protein food and/or moderately flavored dish (as the alcohol gives this wine weight) so not to overwhelm the structure of this varietal. Basic concepts to matching: wine acidity should exceed the food's acidity; the wine's residual sweetness should exceed the food's sweetness; and the weight of the food should match that of the wine. Lighter meats or seafood with *cured* toppings will bond nicely with the fruity sweetness of the wine. Game coated with preserves, soft cheeses and lovely country breads are great accompaniments. Not recommended: A heavy meat or seafood dish as that would drown the wine fruit flavors. And try to stay away from bold, bitter cheeses as they could overwhelm the fruit.

RED VARIETAL FEATURE - MERLOT / BENZIGER

Why MERLOT? This isn't your typical simple fruity drink, but rather a beautiful and powerful expression of Merlot **vinified with an attitude** by Benziger Family Winery. The 2007 Merlot is a little different than 2008, so vintage truly does matter. The 2007 has the perfect grip of controlling masculinity with its velvety but vivid tannins and a sensitive embrace of darker ripened plums, raspberries and currants, and lingering with a touch of clove spice.

...Why not!

All Merlot wines are **not** created equal, and **Benziger Merlot** consistently sets high standards for the palate. The Benziger Family Winery vinifies their wines showcasing the truest expression of the land and the *art of winemaking* creating robust flavors characteristic of the varietal. This Merlot wine is no exception, embracing your palate with luscious black fruits, approachable structure of smooth tannins and balanced acid with a subtle black pepper on the finish. It's a **self-indulging** experience *without* the guilt, just a desire for more.

IF A WINE WERE ME . . .
WHICH WOULD IT BE?

The **Benziger Family Winery** is located in Sonoma Valley, and they are truly about farming the natural way, eliminating the need for chemicals or artificial practices. These practices are reflected in their consistently high quality wines made from a healthy and vibrant land of balanced ecosystems designed for each varietal they grow.

The fruit is handpicked from Sonoma County's Alexander Valley to the Carneros regions, which culminates in the finest quality fruit in each bottle. Have a sip and see why this winery easily has a *dozen awards* of noble **achievement** under its skins. http://www.benziger.com

WHICH WOULD IT BE?

MONTEPULCIANO

CHARACTERISTICS (ATTRIBUTES)	EXPRESSION (PERSONALITIES)	WINE STYLE (STYLE)	FINISH (DEMEANOR)
I am pleasant as a single varietal, and add structure and juiciness to blends of other indigenous varieties. I have naturally soft tannins, due to my thin but pigmented skin, with medium to excited acids, pleasant fruit notes and nice pale to dark ruby hues.	I have a more tempered personality; my scent is deceptive as it is distinct of wild animal-like musk, yet my palate is pleasantly smooth of cherries, berries, and red plums. I have comfortable energetic acidity and am always up for entertaining.	My style is far mellow compared to many of my relatives in Italy, but clearly my loud POV remains - with less tannic structure and juicy red fruits. When in a blend, I provide the backbone and fleshy qualities.	You will find that I'm rather balanced yet provocative, leaving my company with lots to consider. I have been known to linger a bit, but not be disruptive, just engaging. I continue to improve as my acid POV becomes more integrated in my maturity.

Place of origin is central Italy, in Abruzzi and Umbria. The grape varietal is indigenous to Italy and not widely planted or grown outside of there. Montepulciano is vinified dry as a single varietal and in blends with other Italian grapes. The quality of the plantings and vinification has steadily improved over the past decades, and continues to year after year.

Food Styles of **Interest**: If desired, simple good all-around company will work as this varietal is easygoing enough and can hold up to deeper conversation. Assuming that you have chosen wine from this varietal, identify a medium protein food and/or moderately flavored dish to enhance the balanced structure of this varietal. Basic concepts to matching: wine acidity should exceed the food's acidity; the wine's residual sweetness should exceed the food's sweetness; and the weight of the food should match that of the wine. Indulge in marinara-based dish (rice or pasta) or cream-based dishes, such as a primavera risotto; medium meats like lamb, roasted poultry or cerviche; and great Italian cheeses (cave-aged).

IF A WINE WERE ME . . .

WHICH WOULD IT BE?

NEBBIOLO (BAROLO, BARBARESCO)

CHARACTERISTICS (ATTRIBUTES)	EXPRESSION (PERSONALITIES)	WINE STYLE (STYLE)	FINISH (DEMEANOR)
I'm rather exclusive to my origins of Piedmont, and boastful of super firm structure/tannins and screaming acids like most my relatives in this region. Whether as a Barolo or Barberesco, I have aging requirements to help calm my rigid structure and allow my floral and red fruit notes to shine with my pale red hues. I am definitely produced as a single player, I don't have much to do with blending.	People find me a bit abrasive and often defiant because my POV is so vocal. I just like to be heard, but it can be confusing for some. I LOVE being vocal about my attributes of rigid tannins and piercing acids highlighted with red plums, raspberries, earth-mushrooms, rose petals and licorice. I am most intriguing and more balanced with age...you get me at my best with several years under me.	I'm rather obvious with my bold confidence and seemingly flashy style. I love being adorned with oak (old and new). It provides a warm embrace and helps to settle my excitement, but I also will never be dull. I am naturally full of rigor and enthusiasm...it just needs to be channeled and/or some patience to understand me fully.	There is really nothing simplistic about me...my conversations are always thought-provoking and energetic. Once we start the dialogue it doesn't stop as I will leave you with thoughts that linger for a long while, creating interest and challenge at the same time. You need stamina to indulge me, but you won't regret it. Holding on to me is a bonus as I get more exquisite with complex nuances over decades.

Place of origin is Piedmont Italy. The grape varietal is indigenous to Italy and vinified as a dry wine. There are two predominant styles of Nebbiolo (Barolo- the most notable and most astringent and the Barbaresco- more finessed and delicate but still bold); Both styles require 100% nebbiolo grapes to be used when produced. These wines have aging requirements to ensure the acids and tannins have mellowed to an acceptable level before being sold and still can benefit by aging even longer. Nebbiolo grapes create wines of bold character, high acids, tannins, and body, and intriguing red fruits, bitter chocolate and mushroom-like earth in their youth. In maturity, the fruits become more complex of a dried sweeter quality, deeper colored flowers, and the tannins smoothen with less vibrant acids and more of a darker brownish orange (tawny) hue.

WHICH WOULD IT BE?

Food Styles of **Interest**: This is company of great intrigue and adventure...ready to handle the persistence on the palate with ease and interest. When choosing wine from this varietal, identify a heavier protein food and/or boldly flavored dish to match the structure and tannic texture of this varietal. Basic concepts to matching: wine acidity should exceed the food's acidity; the wine's residual sweetness should exceed the food's sweetness; and the weight of the food should match that of the wine. Most bold foods will enhance this wine because of its high acid, high tannins and full structure...go big! Hardy grilled meats, nice flavored bold (aged) cheeses, roasted vegetable casseroles with cheese and bold spices all work well.

IF A WINE WERE ME . . .

WHICH WOULD IT BE?

PINOT NOIR

CHARACTERISTICS (ATTRIBUTES)	EXPRESSION (PERSONALITIES)	WINE STYLE (STYLE)	FINISH (DEMEANOR)
I'm gifted with the natural red fruity sweetness of strawberries and raspberries from my thin skin, and a slight white pepper spice. I provide smooth tannins, medium acidity, and a medium structure with soft red hues. I'm notorious for changing my mind - patience and understanding is a must. I am rarely blended, but will hang with Pinot Meunier and Chardonnay to provide elegance in Champagnes.	I am known to be a bit finicky as I can start out one way and shift plans instantly - but when I am focused I will deliver 100%. I set the bar high and have high expectations; people sometimes perceive this as vain. Did you know there are 3 of us used in traditional Champagne? I'm one of the two reds, the other is Pinot Meunier! I am also praised in the Blanc de Noirs style of Champagne, along with Pinot Meunier.	My style is always a dry wine, however I have mood swings so you have to be willing to accept me in the mood that I'm in. I am tasty in all moods, but just not predictable, which can be exciting. I can be adorned in oak, but you don't want to overdo it as I have so much in my natural offerings that you will mask my greater balanced attributes.	I'm always a proper conversationalist that lingers just the right amount of time. I will not leave you abruptly nor will I outstay my welcome. Most people enjoy being with me as I display a great deal of standards and elegant discipline. I'm great for fine dining and just as good for easy outings - just not simple.

Place of origin is Burgundy, France. Pinot Noir grapes are the more difficult grapes to grow and vinify to the ideal expression, and it takes true understanding of the varietal and what is needed from a viticultural perspective to even get it close. This is often why you can taste a Pinot from different vineyards of the same region and it won't taste the same. Often times there is too much emphasis on vinifying them, but the ideal raw materials aren't there to start with so the expression won't be as it should. Pinot Noir is a delicate grape and is vinified as a single varietal and generally not intended for blending unless for Champagnes. This wine is elegant and structurally well balanced with red fruits and slight white pepper. It sometimes has a bit herbaceous complexity based on the age of the wine, and is designed to drink alone or with foods.

Food Styles of **Interest**: This is really nice, deserving company that you have around for any reason and/or for the finer occasions. For wine from this varietal, identify a medium protein food and/or moderately flavored dish to match the balanced structure and enhance the subtle spiciness of this varietal. Basic concepts to matching: wine acidity should exceed the food's acidity; the wine's residual sweetness should exceed the food's sweetness; and the weight of the food should match that of the wine. Surprisingly, pizza, pasta dishes (cream or marinara-based), salmon or medium meats (not too textured as in grilled) will pair nicely.

WHICH WOULD IT BE?

RED VARIETAL FEATURE - PINOT NOIR / DAVIS FAMILY

Why PINOT NOIR?

I considered not featuring this varietal because it is so well-known, but realized that it is often not truly known in the way that it should be in terms of true varietal expression. I simply *had* to feature the Pinot Noir by **Davis Family Vineyards**. The winery shows their disciplined understanding of cultivating this varietal and bringing out the best of

its characteristics with heart and soul.

This Pinot Noir from the Russian River Valley expresses itself with a balanced and artful integration of acids and smooth tannins, a beautifully *subtle* introduction of raspberry, strawberry and cherry fruit elegance, layered with complex, yet balanced, twists and turns of *spices* that continually swirl on your tongue well after your first sip.

IF A WINE WERE ME . . .

...Why not!

Davis Family Vineyards is a New World producer making fine wines using an Old World style, but with a subtle updated twist. It is evident that they focus their efforts to harvest at ripeness...therefore achieving a perfect balance of sugar, acidity, pH, maturity of flavors and tannins!   This Pinot Noir is like a perfectly **choreographed tango** synchronizing lyrics to movement with its subtle introduction of spice accents and all things nice on the long, swirling finish!

A little info about the winery...**Davis Family Vineyards** is truly run by family with all heart and soul! They perform a balancing balancing act that involves close monitoring of every detail with minimal intervention to allow the flavor of the vineyard to be wholly expressed.

WHICH WOULD IT BE?

They use tradition, technology and science to advance their art. The finishing touches...they age their wines in the finest French oak barrels, just enough to help the wines evolve and to add a subtle seasoning component.

Guy Davis, Founder/Farmer/**Winemaker**.. for whom I have such respect! When I had the fortune of meeting him he was amazingly kind and appreciative of how I personified his wines but they *truly* were expressing personality traits for me. He shared that his winery was a family run operation with his son as the cellar master; he really meant it, as you can see in the picture he is personally into harvesting his grapes. Guy began his artisan winemaking career in the late 80's and furthered his craft by working with some of the best producers in California, and France, as well as Argentina and New Zealand, two regions which he continues to make a wine each year under the "Gusto" label. Davis operates this boutique, artisan, family winery whereby they truly nurture every wine from vine to bottle. The wines are handcrafted with limited supply and available direct from the winery.

"We have strong beliefs about wine and earth-friendly farming, putting our heart and soul into every bottle"
- Guy Davis

http://davisfamilyvineyards.com

WHICH WOULD IT BE?

SANGIOVESE (CHIANTI, BRUNELLO AND VINO NOBILE)

CHARACTERISTICS (ATTRIBUTES)	EXPRESSION (PERSONALITIES)	WINE STYLE (STYLE)	FINISH (DEMEANOR)
I'm quite vocal and known for my racy acidity, aggressive tannins (like many of my Italian relatives in this region), tart red fruits, a bit of earth quality and pale red hues. I'm robust by nature and can be rustic as a single varietal. I am really cool when hanging out and blending with other varietals for Chianti, or for the Super Tuscans experience.	I have multiple personalities based on the clone of me that you are digging. In all cases, you will find me to be of firm structure, with glaring acidity and red fruit notes. I can be the most elegant or the most rustic, and always with a POV.	I represent diversity... your everyday casual sip of goodness with Chianti - a step above as a Vino Nobile di Montepulciano clone, to your premium fine wine of complexity as a Brunello di Montalcino clone. Exquisiteness guaranteed. Additionally, you can have me in a blend, as a sweet passito or Vin Santo, a Rosé or sparkling...however you want me, I can be yours.	You are not likely to forget me in the short term. I can hold a conversation of great depth or just intrigue, but it will rarely be a simple and easily forgotten discussion. I like to entice my audience with stimulating complexity and will do whatever is necessary to strike up a conversation.

Place of origin is Tuscany, Italy. Wines produced from Sangiovese can be as a single varietal or a blend (exceptions are 100% Sangiovese for Brunello as noted above), and are vinfied across the board from dry wines to sparkling and sweet. Sangiovese-based wines have a wide array of characteristics based on where they are vinified, but the constant is firm tannins, high acid, red fruit notes, with a bit of spice (white pepper) and they tend to be light to medium body. In its youth, the cherry notes seem more tart and the acids a bit bold as the wine matures,; the cherry notes are more of a dried sweeter quality and hints of tobacco immerse with dried herbs and earth, melded acids and tannins.

Food Styles of **Interest**: This is for chill company, 'have a glass of wine anytime' Assuming that you have chosen wine from this varietal, identify a higher protein food and/or highly flavored dish to match the full structure, bold acidity and tannins of this varietal. Basic concepts to matching: wine acidity should exceed the food's acidity; the wine's residual sweetness should exceed the food's sweetness; and the weight of the food should match that of the wine. Pasta dishes with marinara sauce (particularly spaghetti and meatballs), pizza, veal or medium meats including seafood based in marinara sauce are good options.

SYRAH / SHIRAZ

CHARACTERISTICS (ATTRIBUTES)	EXPRESSION (PERSONALITIES)	WINE STYLE (STYLE)	FINISH (DEMEANOR)
I'm an adaptable variety, being able to hang solo quite confidently or blend in nicely with others. Solo, I am structured with high tannins and acid, great black fruits and a hint of clove spice with earthy notes and dark red hues. Oak and I get along perfectly. My friends can count on me for support. I'm known for my fruitiness, bold alcohol and bigger body as a Shiraz (either as a single varietal or in blends). Noticeable!	My personality is consistently confident of tannins, outgoing bold acidity and juicy blackberries, blueberries and ripened raspberries with a quick-witted attitude of spice clove or black pepper. I have all the components to blend with anyone - whether outgoing, structured, sharp or reserved...I have it all and I am even more harmonized as I mature.	I can be quite versatile as I am vinified as a dry varietal, in blends, a Rosé, or fortified sweet. With me, you are going to be in good company as I enjoy entertaining and bringing out the best in people. I do so in different ways based on the company, and I am capable of mixing it up with all types and concluding harmoniously. I can be cloaked in oak jewels and still be recognized, and my style continues to improve with age - easily a decade.	You will not soon forget me, in my youth or maturity. I am loaded with juiciness, excitement and fulfilling structure to engage a conversation and keep it going. I can be smooth or throw you a curve ball - you have to know what you are after. In my maturity, way more complexity surfaces with the sophistication that you may not have noticed, so hang with me as I make your wait worthwhile.

Place of origin is Rhone Valley, France and *known* as **Shiraz** in Australia, but grown in many parts around the world (Washington, California, New Zealand, South Africa, etc.). Syrah is generally vinified dry in France and, of notable quality, as a single varietal in Northern Rhone as well as bold and elegant as a blending component to Grenache and Mourvedre in Southern Rhone.

I F   A   W I N E   W E R E   M E . . .

Based on the soils and climate where Syrah/Shiraz is grown and the technique used to vinify it, the characteristics will differ. In moderate climates, the wine is more tannic and the spice notes are more pronounced of coarse black pepper and fresh black fruits of plums, blackberry and blueberries (more prominent taste in the New World style of wines), and often chocolate notes. In hot climates, the tannins are more velvety and spice becomes more complex of clove with ripened black fruit profiles with some raspberry notes, and mushroom quality of earth and leather on the finish. The color is more of a crimson red.

Shiraz in Australia is vinified with more diversity in style and most commonly with a juicy fruitier focus as a dry single varietal and a full body rosé, fortified sweet.

Food Styles of **Interest**: This is company for any occasion and definitely those needing a bite to eat with their drink. When selecting wine of this varietal, identify a higher protein food and/or moderate to highly flavored dish to match this full structured, bold acidity and tannic-driven varietal. Basic concepts to matching: wine acidity should exceed the food's acidity; the wine's residual sweetness should exceed the food's sweetness; and the weight of the food should match that of the wine. Suggestions: savory meats, a panini sandwich with eggplant or medium meat, pasta with heavy flavored marinara sauce, and bold hard aged cheeses.

I F   A   W I N E   W E R E   M E . . .

TEMPRANILLO

CHARACTERISTICS (ATTRIBUTES)	EXPRESSION (PERSONALITIES)	WINE STYLE (STYLE)	FINISH (DEMEANOR)
I am known as many different names; I have a knack for blending with others of fruity quality. I'm naturally stoic being of firm tannins due to my thick skins. Sometimes it's hard to detect my sweet fruity aromas through my toughness but they exist along with my ruby red hues.	I am a pretty straight forward no-nonsense structure of tight tannins, including a glimpse of red plums and strawberries, and not very vocal acidity. You will generally appreciate me in blends as my friends love the support I provide as an anchor for them, and they balance me out with their sweeter and energetic qualities.	My style is generally dry, and as a blend as I'm a great companion. On occasion you will find me as a single varietal with fresh red fruit notes and easy going. You can also find me as one of the fortified blends of Port wines, known by the name Tinta Roriz.	It's easy to have a conversation with me and/or one of my friends as we make the topics tempered. While I certainly have a structured perspective, I get along well with others. I'm rather easygoing and not too racy...I make for an easy sip of everyday youthfulness.

Place of origin, Rioja Spain (and central). Wines produced from Tempranillo tend to be full bodied with solid tannins, moderate to low acidity, red fruit notes of red plums and berries, often hints of tobacco or dust, vanilla bean accent and ruby red hues.

Food Styles of **Interest:** This is for any and all kinds of company that enjoy entertaining and being entertained. Assuming that you have chosen wine of this varietal, identify a higher protein food and/or highly flavored dish to match the full structure and firm tannins of this varietal. Basic concepts to matching: wine acidity should exceed the food's acidity (this wine is low in acidity); the wine's residual sweetness should exceed the food's sweetness; and the weight of the food should match that of the wine. Nice pairings include medium meats like poultry, pork or lamb, medium firm cheeses, or cheese lasagna with the Rioja style of this varietal. Also consider more prominent powerful meats/dishes like grilled meats or calamari, pasta and cream sauce, and aged hard cheeses for the Ribera del Duero style.

IF A WINE WERE ME...

RED VARIETAL FEATURE - TEMPRANILLO / TEMPUS ALBA

Why Tempranillo?

This varietal is quite bold and hearty, and displays balance when vinified with careful attention to its natural bones-driven structure. With Tempus Tempranillo, you will be pleased with the result of their long precise fermentation processes, which reveals more depth and usual structure of expression from this varietal. Their process results in a darker red color with complex aromas of fresh red and dark fruits, with a **controlled palate** of structure and finesse.

I F   A   W I N E   W E R E   M E . . .

... Why Not!

Tempus Alba is part of the genesis of a new way of wine making in Argentina. They aim to capture the passion for what they do in each of the wines offered, and this bold Tempranillo is no exception. It renders their passion in the bottle with its complex attack of concentrated blackberries and black plums, firm tannins melding with energetic acidity, and bundled in a pleasant finish of vanilla and clove spices. This is **complexity at its finest.**

Tempus Alba is a **Dogma Winery** dedicated to the highest quality of wine making by keeping productions small, never exceeding more than 300,000 liters in total premium production per year.

Grapes used in the production of their wines come from their own vineyards, guaranteeing consistency in quality and finesse of the terroir from vintage to vintage.

IF A WINE WERE ME . . .

WHICH WOULD IT BE?

ZINFANDEL / PRIMITIVO

CHARACTERISTICS (ATTRIBUTES)	EXPRESSION (PERSONALITIES)	WINE STYLE (STYLE)	FINISH (DEMEANOR)
I am definitely a solo player with my rich juicy fruit notes, medium to full body and boozy alcohol, solid tannins and crimson red hues. I like to stand out and, whether in Italy or California, my traits stay consistently bold. I am good for several years, but not too much longer or my taste profile will tire.	I'm the outgoing type...I love having a good time and being the life of the party with my energetic acids, bold tannins, and luscious red and black berry fruits. I am all-around confident in what I have to offer and enjoy entertaining.	Most consider me to be versatile and I would agree. I can be excitable and energetic to elegant and balanced. I am vinified as a dry/still wine, in blends, as a Rosé, or sweet wine. It is for certain that you will recognize my boozy alcohol attributes whether as a Primitivo or Zinfandel.	Gregarious and long lasting...my conversations can go on forever but ensured a good time! I can go deep and be provocative or just keep the dialogue going at any level. I am good company at any type of event just let me know what you need and I will adapt.

Place of origin for Primitvo is Puglia, Italy although Zinfandel is reputed as a California grape - Zinfandel and Primitivo are the same varietal. Zinfandel/ Primitivo wines are generally vinified dry as single varietals and in blends. They are medium to full body, and taste will vary across California's vast regions - from concentrated or overly ripened dark berry and raspberry fruits with clove or anise spice *to* vibrant fresh fruit notes with spice of pepper, medium acidity, bold tannins and boozy with crimson red hues. Primitivo select old vineyards express jammy fruits balanced with bold acids and are just as boozy as Californian Zinfandel.

Food Styles of **Interest**: This is best for good all-around people that like to celebrate with big palates *and* food! For wine of this varietal, identify a higher protein food and/or highly flavored dish to match the full structure, bold acidity and tannins of this varietal. Basic concepts to matching: wine acidity should exceed the food's acidity; the wine's residual sweetness should exceed the food's sweetness; and the weight of the food should match that of the wine. This is a great wine for BBQ foods or grilled meats (the texture of these foods will enhance the wine).

I F   A   W I N E   W E R E   M E . . .
WHICH WOULD IT BE?

BLENDING: REDS BENEFIT FROM WHITES

Basically, wines from different grapes are blended to achieve more depth and complexity of flavors, texture and structure. The goal of blending wines (red or white) made in different vintages is more to balance out the flavor characteristics.

In some cases, the winemaker will blend whites with reds in order to create the best possible combination of aromas and flavors. White grapes are a great addition for making different styles of red wines, there are different qualities and attributes of the white grape variety that helps the red wine to express subtle nuances. There are several examples of the wine-made magic in blending both red and white varietals.

- Côte-Rôtie in France northern Rhone Valley region, blends the red spicy and firm structured Syrah varietal with the aromatic softer fruitier Viognier ...this is a drinkable art of a floral, spicy blend.

- Hermitage or Crozes Hermitage, also in the Rhone Valley blends the earthy tannic Syrah with the more fruitier white varietals of Rousanne for floral astringency and acidity, and Marsanne providing opulent body, pear fruit and nuttiness. Resulting in a sultry, more elegant drink of combined attributes.

- Or the most common result of Champagne, the blend of two red varietals Pinot Noir (for structure and fruit), Pinot Meunier (for floral notes and fruit) with one white varietal, Chardonnay (for acidity mostly) another superb experience.

While it is more common to experience reds blended with other reds and the same can be said for whites with whites than it is to see the cross blending of red and white. In all cases the goal of the winemaker is to design the *balance* of flavors, structure (acids and tannins), alcohol and other characteristics to create an exciting taste and aromatic result.

WINE SPEAK - SPARKLING

IF A WINE WERE ME...
WHICH WOULD IT BE?

SPARKLING WINES

Simply put, Sparkling Wines are basically still wines with CO_2.gas which creates bubbles / carbonation. Under the category of sparklers, there are many styles, most notably Champagne (with various styles), Crémant, Spumante (with various styles), Cava, Sekt, Sparkling Wines, Rosé Sparkling Wines, and so on.

VINIFICATION - METHODS

There are four different techniques used to produce sparkling wines resulting in different textures (mouthfeel), CO_2 levels of pressure, size of bubbles, flavor profiles, etc. To give you an idea of which style might be akin to your personality, below is a description of the methods used so that you may consider the level of complexity that best suits you.

The Traditional Method (Champagne Methode): This is a rigorous method including two fermentations. The first fermentation is much like making still white wines, except that *the winemaker will leverage grapes harvested with the highest acid levels and least sugar.* A second fermentation then takes place in the same bottle in which yeast is added, along with a determined amount of sugar for pressure, and then capped off from air to allow the CO_2 gas pressure to build naturally. The yeast cells will eventually eat up the sugar and die (lees) inside the bottle, giving the unique characteristics and bread-like qualities tasted in the finished product. This is after a determined minimum period of time - 15 months for Non-Vintage Champagne and 36 months for Vintage Champagne, while other regions have their minimum time requirements as well. After this time period, the lees has to be gathered (riddling) and removed through a painstaking process (disgorgement). Then, a sweet mixture, along with some of the base wine, is added to top off the bottle (the process is called dosage) and is a determinant for the sweetness level of the final product before it is corked and the wire cage added for double sealing measures.

These sparkling wines are more superior and higher quality produced wines, with all possible complexities available for your palate.

The Transfer Method: This is the same as the traditional method above **except** after the second fermentation the wine is processed in a tank with CO_2 under pressure, bulk filtered (controlling consistency in quality), and then bottled again in different bottles.

These sparkling wines are good quality produced wines and often provide less yeasty flavors on your palate.

The **Charmat / Tank Method**: This process involves a first fermentation as described above; *however,* the second fermentation occurs in stainless steel tanks (so not to add flavors or oxygen) then filtered and bottled under pressure.

These sparking wines capture fresher flavors and less yeasty notes, and are great for aromatic varietal focused wines, as in the Prosecco style.

Carbonation Injection: This method involves injecting CO_2 into the wine, much like soda pop is produced.

These sparkling wines are of lesser quality and create more coarse and inconsistent bubbles which dissipate almost immediately.

SPARKLING WINES KEY: (*the least taste of sweetness - to the most taste of sweetness*)

Brut Natural/ Extra Brut = least sweet/ extra 'dry';

Brut = dry;

Extra Dry (not to be confused with Extra Brut) = dryer than sec sweeter than brut;

Sec = a little sweet;

Demi Sec = sweeter than sec, half dry / half sweet;

Doux = very sweet, more of a dessert wine.

Rosé Spumante "Osè" Sparkling demi-sec wine

IF A WINE WERE ME . . .
WHICH WOULD IT BE?

STYLES OF SPARKLING WINES

CHAMPAGNE - both a region *and* style of sparking wine in France; the region is exclusively for production of sparkling wines made in the traditional method or methode Champeneoise. Only sparkling wines made in Champagne can be labeled as such. Champagnes is a blend of up to three varietals, most commonly Pinot Noir (for structure and fruit quality), Chardonnay (for citrus and elegance quality) and Pinot Meunier (for aromatics quality).

Styles **of** Champagne:

STYLES OF	CHARACTERISTICS (ATTRIBUTES)	EXPRESSION (PERSONALITY)	WINE STYLE (STYLE)	FINISH (DEMEANOR)
Prestige Cuvée	I have the finest sips of everything wonderful, and tastes are harmonized with varying levels of intensity that last forever. My grapes are of premium quality - the best that 'the house' can purchase or grow. – and sure to be impressive.	I have exemplary flavor, both refined and complex – yes, I am one hell of an occasion! Prim and proper in a traditional yet exciting sense, I am of the finest caliber and proud of it. I have every bit of balanced complexity with my fruits, nuts, baked bread, and citrus flavors and full body. I expect attention and keep exclusive company...only those who are part of my inner circle.	I am exquisitely powerful and balanced. You get nothing but the best with me, and my social network reflects my values of excellence. As I am a blend, you should expect the ultimate expression of the three of us.	My repertoire of conversation is endless. I can engage you at any level and on any topic, and leaving you with provocative yet pleasant thoughts that will linger. The finest of times are to be appreciated with me!

I F   A   W I N E   W E R E   M E . . .

STYLES OF	CHARACTERISTICS (ATTRIBUTES)	EXPRESSION (PERSONALITY)	WINE STYLE (STYLE)	FINISH (DEMEANOR)
Vintage	Prestigious, in a word. I represent what is unique about the year, and my qualities support the distinctions beautifully and boldly. I am rarely planned but deliver astounding results. I proudly share my unique qualities with others, like the non-vintage.	I am 'special' in that I'm produced only from years of great difference. You will know me because I will be labeled with my vintage (year). I can be complex in flavor, which often includes dried fruits, nuts, floral notes, and creamy tones due to minimum aging requirements. I am well worth a NICE celebration.	I am best described as one-of-a-kind. My diverse style is dependent on what the vintage expressed. I can display most intriguing quality, but know that I will always stand out with distinction! I enjoy being uniquely expressed.	I can be a challenge as you don't know exactly what you will get in conversation with me, but you know that it will be unique, distinguished and complex. My conversation is sure to linger with intrigue...curiosity is paramount with me.
Non Vintage	Good to meet me, I'm sure. I am casual enough to be appreciated for any occa sion; proper enough to hang around the highest class of company and chill enough to fulfill the average crowd. I am adaptable and enjoy a reason to celebrate with company.	I am consistent in my ways - after all, I represent the 'House' blend. I can range from crisp and medium to full and creamy with nuts, biscuits, and dried fruits, dependent on my producer. I, too, have minimum age requirements. I am of solid quality - good for most anytime.	You can count on me to be consistent and work well with most. I am vinified with varying levels of dryness. I will not disappoint as I am always excited about hanging out and being a part of the entertainment, but not too demanding.	My conversations are generally well articulated and never too extreme unless you get me going. My thoughts may linger a bit longer than expected but they will be good ones! I'm all about enjoyment and that is what you should expect with me.

I F   A   W I N E   W E R E   M E . . .
WHICH WOULD IT BE?

STYLES OF	CHARACTERISTICS (ATTRIBUTES)	EXPRESSION (PERSONALITY)	WINE STYLE (STYLE)	FINISH (DEMEANOR)
Rosé	I am a fine sip of pink (pale to dark red) and love being the center of attention with my varying hues of pink and red. I provide choices of depth and flavor concentration based on the varietals used and the method by which I am produced.	I can be quite diverse based on how I'm produced and what varietals are used. You may find me complex in structure and deep in thought or simple red fruitiness and energetic with lots of citrus to excite. But most of all you will find the consistency of my red fruits.	I am vinified with varying levels of dryness - dry (minimal sweetness) through doux (sweet), still to sparkling and somewhere in-between. I am always strutting some pleasant shade of pink or red, so you couldn't possibly miss seeing me.	I am great at creating awareness around me and keeping the conversation going even when a simple topic. I am good at calling attention to myself and enjoy holding the audience captive...pure bliss!
Blanc de Blancs (white of white grapes)	I'm an elegant and velvety sip. You will notice a nice smooth mouthfeel, even with the subtle yet intriguing nuances I display. You will only find me as a white grape varietal, usually Chardonnay, with structure and balance.	It's always a smooth time with me, often resulting in a creamy, light-medium body with gentle crisp citrus and vibrant fruit. I am great for any occasion with balanced effervescence, and never a disappointment. In my age, my flavors are more integrated, creating an even smoother texture.	I am designed as a dry sparkling wine, and you may find me with varying levels of residual fruit sweetness but hardly noticeable. I am always composed and soothing to be around with my engaging warmth.	You will find nothing but the smoothest conversation and tone with me. I am usually passionate and show my excitement with consistency. I invite serenity with each sip...I'm a delicate pleasure!

STYLES OF	CHARACTERISTICS (ATTRIBUTES)	EXPRESSION (PERSONALITY)	WINE STYLE (STYLE)	FINISH (DEMEANOR)
Blanc de Noirs (white of black grapes)	I'm generally structured and complex given that I'm a sparkling wine made of black grape varieties. You will find that my talents are displayed differently based on the varietals chosen and the amount of time spent macerating on my skins. I like to think of myself as medium body and pronounced taste.	I am made from black grapes only (generally pinot noir and pinot meunier), resulting in a fuller structured body with pronounced berry fruit qualities and rounded mouthfeel. I am versatile and my effervescence makes me enjoyable for any occasion.	I am most always a dry sparkling wine with a strong view on complexity with balance. I love that my softer pale orange pink hues can be a bit deceptive to the palate as there is nothing soft about me...I'm full body and daring. Enjoy being the life of the party!	My conversational range is broad and you are never left with a dull moment. I bring a bit of mystique to the table and can linger for a while as you discover the subtle distinctions about me. .I am all heart and soul, and love to engage in healthy discussions.

Food Styles of **Interest**:

Tete de Cuvée – This is for entertaining great company with the best and/or for any celebratory reason - not that you really need one. Assuming that you've chosen this type of sparkling wine to pair with food, identify which style will suit your meal best. Basic concepts to matching: wine acidity should exceed the food's acidity; the wine's residual sweetness should exceed the food's sweetness; and the weight of the food should match that of the wine. Pairing considerations include delicate foods such as caviar, soft mild cheeses, smoked fish and chocolate desserts.

Vintage – This is for entertaining great company with exquisiteness and/or for any celebratory reason - not that you really need one. Assuming that you have chosen this type of sparkling wine to pair with food, identify which style will suit your meal best. Basic concepts to matching: wine acidity should exceed the food's acidity; the wine's residual sweetness should exceed the food's sweetness; and the weight of the food should match that of the wine. Consider oysters, caviar, mushroom-based dishes (rice, pasta, etc.), grilled seafood, fish cakes and chocolate- covered fruits.

NV (non vintage) – This is for entertaining good company with excellence and/or for any celebratory reason, - not that you really need one. Assuming that you've chosen this type of sparkling wine to pair with food, identify which style will suit your meal best. Basic concepts to matching: wine acidity should exceed the food's acidity; the wine's residual sweetness should exceed the food's sweetness; and the weight of the food should match that of the wine. Food considerations for brut wines include Thai, seafood, fried foods, ceviche and mushroom-based dishes (rice, pasta, etc.).

I F A W I N E W E R E M E . . .
WHICH WOULD IT BE?

Rosé – This is for entertaining all types of fun company with excellence and/ or for any celebratory reason - not that you really need one. Assuming that you have chosen this type of sparkling wine to pair with food, identify which style will suit your meal best. Basic concepts to matching: wine acidity should exceed the food's acidity; the wine's residual sweetness should exceed the food's sweetness; and the weight of the food should match that of the wine. Good food options include cured meats, smoked fish, soft cheese (brie or goat cheese), chocolate-coated fruits and chocolate desserts.

Blanc de Noirs - This is for entertaining all types of fun company with structured sparkling and/or for any celebratory reason - not that you really need one. Assuming that you have chosen this type of sparkling wine to pair with food, identify which style will suit your meal best. Basic concepts to matching: wine acidity should exceed the food's acidity; the wine's residual sweetness should exceed the food's sweetness; and the weight of the food should match that of the wine. Pairing considerations include poultry and seafood, both textured and with or without sauce, to compare with the structured elements of the wine.

Blanc de Blancs – This is for entertaining all types of fun company with delicacy and/or for any celebratory reason - not that you really need one. Assuming that you have chosen this type of sparkling wine to pair with food, identify which style will suit your meal best. Basic concepts to matching: wine acidity should exceed the food's acidity; the wine's residual sweetness should exceed the food's sweetness; and the weight of the food should match that of the wine. Considerations include potato-based dishes (fried or casseroles), delicate mushroom based dishes, and Asian foods mellow with the creamy nature of the wine. Strong cheeses cut through the creaminess.

SPARKLING WINE FEATURE - Osè Rosé / TENUTE TOMASELLA

Why Rosé Sparkling?

This is a style that has not been much appreciated over the years, but lately it has been finding its way to popularity This style has waffled in and out of popularity *or* has been vinified as a sweet mess (unless liked that way), particularly with some of the new world style wines. However, thanks to wineries like **Tenute Tomasella** which dared to resuscitate the demi-sec rosé sparkling, this one provides a strong identity with its elegant and sustained taste profile of minimal sweetness and approachable complexity.

...**Why not**! In just a few words, this gorgeous Osé rosé sparkling wine is intriguing and harmonized, expressing **pleasant assuredness** on the palate! You are left with remnants of red fruit, dark rose pedals, nice balanced citrus spark, and an intriguing taste of roasted espresso beans, finishing like velvet on your tongue for a good long while. If not obvious, this *is* an **exquisite and impressionable rosé** from Tenute Tomasella Winery. They use Refosco and Verduzzo grapes, withered on the plant, which provide a more complex structure while displaying the perfect balance between sweetness and acidity.

This winery began pairing Osè with food and dishes from all over the world, creating unexpected, incredibly harmonious and delicious combinations acknowledged and confirmed by many wine critics.

WHICH WOULD IT BE?

By producing this Rosé 'drinkable art', the winery has achieved great harmony and balance in a unique cuvée combining Friuli Verduzzo for the softness, intense aroma and texture. Refosco, offering the rosé color due to a short maceration on its skins, adds the perfect amount of acidity and freshness. This is a versatile year round drink of awesomeness.

I F   A   W I N E   W E R E   M E . . .

WHICH WOULD IT BE?

Aside from the amazing sensation on the palate experienced with this wine, its particular organoleptic qualities make this great sparkling wine a versatile companion for dried, sweet, creamy, and even salty foods.

"TOP ONE HUNDRED WINES FROM ITALY 2012", by Paolo Massobrio and Marco Gatti

IF A WINE WERE ME . . .

WHICH WOULD IT BE?

STYLES OF	CHARACTERISTICS (ATTRIBUTES)	EXPRESSION (PERSONALITY)	WINE STYLE (STYLE)	FINISH (DEMEANOR)
CRÉMANT (*using methode champenoise to make sparklers in Europe, just not located in Champagne*)	Generally speaking, I have a nice creamy mouthfeel, and I can be complex with excitable acids and biscuit flavors, balanced structure and varying fruit flavors (fresh apples, peaches, apricots and often dried figs), based on where I'm produced.	I am all about enveloping you with my creamy embrace; I love to balance out my crisp acids with a softer texture that relaxes the palate with citrus fruit flavors and nuances like dried fruits, and sometimes a subtle hint of spice.	I am generally vinified dry or as a Rosé. My approach to most things is with a solid yet soft touch. I am as energetic as the next, but not as obvious because I approach things with a tenderness and always in good taste.	I'm often mistaken for easygoing because of my smooth conversational nature, but don't be fooled. I have a strong POV and can linger in a conversation as long as anyone. I like to keep things cozy and highly enjoyable.
CAVA	I am produced in Spain using the traditional method with mostly indigenous grapes. My taste has medium excitement from acids and often distinct smokiness (from the break down of yeast cells).	I am all about being original, evident by my use of grapes like Macabeu, Xarel-lo and others. I am rather balanced with my enthusiasm and medium body, but you may notice the different taste with my indigenous grape subtleties.	My style is generally dry (with varying levels of dryness). You can also find me as a rosé with fruitier grapes like Garnacha. Sometimes my stature can seem a bit intimidating but my energy is tame. I am well enjoyed with good company.	I can hold a simple conversation or one of much length and provocation. I like to be constantly balanced in my enthusiasm, and that is dependent upon how I'm vinified. I can seem a bit rough around the edges sometimes, but nonetheless, I'm an enjoyable sip.

I F   A   W I N E   W E R E   M E . . .
WHICH WOULD IT BE?

STYLES OF	CHARACTERISTICS (ATTRIBUTES)	EXPRESSION (PERSONALITY)	WINE STYLE (STYLE)	FINISH (DEMEANOR)
SPUMANTE (fully sparkling) **FRIZZANTE (semi-sparkling)**	I am produced in Italy, and my natural tendencies will range from simple, light, fruity and vibrant to full, vibrant and complex due to my aging requirements (bringing focus to my depth and subtle nuances).	I like to be noticed, whether for my easy drinking fruity sweetness - fresh melon and apple fruits with an energetic attitude of acids - to my more contemplative and focused nature. I have many ways of expressing myself as you can see, you only need to know what you want in me.	My style is wide ranging including simple, no-nonsense sweet fruity goodness as an Asti which you can sip on all day and hardly notice. As a Prosecco, I have a light freshness of floral scents, fruits and light body. I can also be deeply contemplative of bigger body, with complex fruit flavors and citrus peel, bold acids and full body as a Franciacorta, or a finessed Trento from aging requirements.	You can get quite a bit of attitude with me, but I am always enjoyable. Know that whatever you experience it will be memorable - whether the conversation goes into the wee hours of the night or ends rather soon, it will be yummy goodness.

IF A WINE WERE ME . . .
WHICH WOULD IT BE?

STYLES OF	CHARACTERISTICS (ATTRIBUTES)	EXPRESSION (PERSONALITY)	WINE STYLE (STYLE)	FINISH (DEMEANOR)
SEKT	I am mostly produced using the Charmat Method in Germany; my flavors will be better noticed and my level of energy keeps things exciting. My greatness depends upon the varietals chosen, but I will be interesting and always teeming with excitement.	I like to sport my diversity of racy acidity to full structured floral with red fruits. I strive for balance but a lot depends on the varietals I'm made of and the company you find me with. I am a good all-around sip.	My style is quite versatile and I like to please, so you only need to decide if you want fresh, citrusy and energetic or more balanced, floral and structured. I am pretty easy going.	You will find my conversations vary from light hearted and enthusiastic to more provocative and deeply engaged. I am always working to keep things interesting so you will have that for certain.
SPARKLING WINES - American and other	I am the broadest category, reflecting diversity and style and produced in all regions around the world. There is not a standard for me as my production can range from traditional method to that of carbonation injection. My tastes are just as broad based on the region producing me and the varietals used.	I am versatile and there is a side to me that will get along with anyone...you only need to determine how you want me to display. I can have the most fine, delicate bubble to the largest coarse excitement.	I'm all about versatility as you can have whatever you want with me. I can be displayed in all styles, including all levels of dryness and from any place in the world. You want a style, I'm it!	Your experience with me will depend on which region you landed on and how I was produced. In all cases, I will have a level of enthusiasm, and assume good-to-great conversation just because I am a sparkling wine.

I F   A   W I N E   W E R E   M E . . .
WHICH WOULD IT BE?

Food Styles of **Interest**:

CRÉMANT – This is for entertaining all types of fun company for amazing mouthfeel experiences and/or for any celebratory reason - not that you really need one. Assuming that you have chosen this type of sparkling wine to pair with food, identify which style will suit your meal best. Basic concepts to matching: wine acidity should exceed the food's acidity; the wine's residual sweetness should exceed the food's sweetness; and the weight of the food should match that of the wine. Considerations include soft cheeses, smoked fish, pickled condiments, and fruit and nut desserts.

CAVA – This is for entertaining all types of fun company for excitement and/or for any celebratory reason, not that you really need one. Assuming that you've chosen this type of sparkling wine to pair with food, identify which style will suit your meal best. Basic concepts to matching: wine acidity should exceed the food's acidity; the wine's residual sweetness should exceed the food's sweetness; and the weight of the food should match that of the wine. Pairing considerations include cerviche, fried foods, Caesar salad, vegetable chips (sweet potato and potato) and fruit tarts.

SPUMANTE – This is for entertaining all types of fun company with enthusiasm and/or for any celebratory reason - not that you have chosen this type of sparkling wine to pair with food, identify which style will suit your meal best. Basic concepts to matching: wine acidity should exceed the food's acidity; the wine's residual sweetness should exceed the food's sweetness; and the weight of the food should match that of the wine. Food considerations include soft cheeses (brie) or cave-aged blue, biscotti biscuits, fruits, nuts and cheesecake.

SEKT – This is for entertaining all types of fun company with excitement and/ or for any celebratory reason, not that you really need one. Assuming that you have chosen this type of sparkling wine to pair with food, identify which style will suit your meal best. Basic concepts to matching: wine acidity should exceed the food's acidity; the wine's residual sweetness should exceed the food's sweetness; and the weight of the food should match that of the wine. Considerations include scallops, lobster, sushi and mushroom-based dishes.

AMERICAN SPARKLING WINES & OTHER– This is for entertaining all types of fun company with excellence and/or for any celebratory reason - not that you really need one. Assuming that you have chosen this type of sparkling wine to pair with food, identify which style will suit your meal best. Basic concepts to matching: wine acidity should exceed the food's acidity; the wine's residual sweetness should exceed the food's sweetness; and the weight of the food should match that of the wine. Considerations include seafood, sushi, poultry, mushroom-based dishes (rice or pasta), cheeses, fried foods (as it cuts through the fat and compares the texture), cheesecake and butter cookies.

WINE SPEAK - DESSERT

I F   A   W I N E   W E R E   M E . . .
WHICH WOULD IT BE?

DESSERT WINES - FORTIFIED / NON-FORTIFIED

Simply stated, fortified wines include the addition of spirit (booze). These wines have a minimum requirement of 15% abv (alcohol by volume). Fortified wines are produced in varying styles: dry (not sweet), semi-dry (slightly sweet with noticeable residual sugar), and sweet.

Non-Fortified wines do not have spirit added to them and have a delicious taste of pure classic dessert wine. These wines have a minimum requirement of 15% abv as well.

VINIFICATION METHODS

Fortified wines are made by adding booze, (a spirit like brandy) to the wine before, during or after fermentation, resulting in different styles and, in all cases, disrupting the fermentation process. The styles of fortified wines will vary and indicated below:

Sweet wines result when the spirit is added before or during the fermentation process, increasing the alcohol level and leaving quite a bit of residual sugar.
Examples of **Sweet** fortified wines include Madeira, Port, Cream Sherry (Pedro Ximenez / PX, Cream Sherry),
Vins doux Naturels / VDN, Vin de Liqueur (sweeter than VDN as the booze is added prior to fermentation), etc

Dry fortified styles occur when the spirit is added after the wine has fully fermented dry, which causes increased alcohol and no sweetness.
Examples of **dry** fortified wines wines include Sherry Fino (dry style), Marsala, Madeira (dry style), Port (dry style), etc.

Semi-dry styles result from stopping the fermentation process to the measured degree of residual sweetness desired.
Examples of **semi-dry/medium-dry** fortified wines include Port, Madeira, etc

Non-fortified wines are produced when there isn't any spirit added to the wine to increase its alcohol; instead, the sweetness level is achieved by stopping the natural yeast fermentation process before completely dry, leaving the desired level of residual sugar sweetness in the wine. This natural process of leveraging concentrated flavors from the grape is derived from various methods, resulting in different styles and body / structure. Making wines in the style of non-fortified are:

- **Noble rot** (a good fungus named botrytis cinerea) grows on the skin of the grape and, believe it or not, is actually beneficial as it dehydrates the grape and enhances it with the effect of dried fruits and honey – this results in a natural amazingly **concentrated flavor** of sweetness and luscious texture. The sugar levels from these concentrated grapes are so high, and the alcohol level achieved is naturally high causing self termination of fermentation with **substantial alcohol and sweetness**. This is why this type of non-fortified wines is the premium quality product. *Examples* of wines produced by this method include Sauterne from the Bordeaux region, Loupiac, Monbazillac made in other French regions, Tokaji Aszu from Hungary, and Beerenauslese from Germany.

- **Grapes frozen** on the vine are actually picked frozen and fermented as is with the iced water removed during pressing of the grapes. This helps retain a highly concentrated level of sweetness which, in turn, (much like the noble rot) kills off the yeast naturally and terminates fermentation when the yeast can no longer survive. The result is a sweet wine with often **lower alcohol**. *Examples* of wines produced by this method include Eiswein in Germany, and Icewine in Canada and New York..

- **Grapes dried** after harvesting involve removing the water from healthy grapes by developing a concentrated dried fruit flavor, much like sweet complex raisins. *Examples* of wines produced by this method include Vin Santo and Passito wines, and Recioto della Valipolicella from different regions in Italy.

WHICH WOULD IT BE?

DESSERT / FORTIFIED WINES

Port

Madeira

Vin de Liqueur

I F   A   W I N E   W E R E   M E . . .
WHICH WOULD IT BE?

FORTIFIED WINES

WHICH WOULD IT BE?

MADEIRA

STYLES OF	CHARACTERISTICS (ATTRIBUTES)	EXPRESSION (PERSONALITIES)	WINE STYLE (STYLE)	FINISH (DEMEANOR)
Dry, Semi-dry, Medium Sweet, Sweet	I am from a beautiful Portuguese island (Madeira) off the coast of Morocco. I am interesting and complex yet still balanced. I am composed of various different grape varieties from all over my island and create just as much diversity on the palate from dry (Sercial) through sweetest (Malmsey) with Bual and Verdelho in between. Be careful with my deliciousness as I have just as much booziness.	My historical and unique way of being vinified (aged through the hottest section of export ships), has made me a rare and amazingly sturdy quality. I am capable of handling adversity - just have a look at my past and how I continue to persevere with greatness of dried figs, citrus peel, roasted nuts and clove spices. You will find me to be of elegant complexity and impressive company.	I am versatile in style from dry to sweet and everything in between. I am quite rare and pleased to share my ways with others. I can be quite mysterious or prominent...it just depends on your interests. I am that fine sip of better - truly the ageless beauty.	There is never a dull or simple moment with me. I am all about interest and intrigue, quite dynamic naturally and full of great stories. My conversations continue to stay with you long after I've left. All things stimulating is what I am!

Food Styles of **Interest**: Be selfish with this delightful drink or, if you have to, go ahead and indulge **good** company. When choosing this wine to pair with food, identify which style will suit your meal best. Basic concepts to matching: wine acidity should exceed the food's acidity (all Madeira styles have medium to high acidity); the wine's residual sweetness should exceed the food's sweetness (Malmsey-sweet will be the sweetest style while Bual and Verdelho will have some level of sweetness); and the weight of the food should match that of the wine (medium plus to full body in all styles)

All that said, with the Sercial dry style, consider contrasting it with something savory like roasted game, stew, or a nut-based tart. For Verdelho and Bual (medium dry), consider slightly salted roasted nuts (filbert, walnuts and/or almonds), an assortment of flavorful cheeses, a nut-based and dried fruit tart. With Malmsey (sweet), consider ice cream, a nut and dried fruit tart like apricots and almonds, or chocolate. It's clearly a perfect drink all by itself too when slightly chilled.

I F A W I N E W E R E M E . . .
WHICH WOULD IT BE?

FORTIFIED WINE FEATURE - MADEIRA / THE RARE WINE CO & BARBEITO

Why Madeira? It is everything one could hope for in a drink and more, a wine of **tremendous character** and harmonized flavors, plus choices, choices, choices as it is produced in every style from dry to sweet. While attending a Madeira tasting I had the great fortune of meeting the man behind the revival of the Madeira status in the U.S., Mannie Berk. It was an honor to hear his wealth of knowledge on the subject of Madeira as well as his insights as a top Importer of rare wines.

I tasted wines from three to 100 years old...no joke! The 1912 Madeira was the famed one for me, and I can only imagine what his 1720 vintage bottle tastes like. The 1912 was markedly energetic, yet possessed a harmonized bouquet of flavors from beautifully dried sweet fruits, a mixture of walnuts and almonds, and citrus peel, to a hint of tobacco and cinnamon spice on the elegant never ending finish. This was a truly *euphoric experience*...the wonder and balance of 100 years of **magnificence in a bottle!** Ponder that for a moment.

I F   A   W I N E   W E R E   M E . . .
WHICH WOULD IT BE?

Even if you never meet Mannie Berk of The Rare Wine Company you can still experience his influence and elegant taste in Madeira through his partnership with Vinhos Barbeito, one of his suppliers. They have teamed up to produce blends with the rich flavors and subtle bouquet of older Madeira wines in the surprisingly affordable Historic Series:

http://www.rarewineco.com/html/rwc-hist.htm   http://www.vinhosbarbeito.com

...Why Not! The beauty of Madeira is beyond its versatility - these wines are of a majestic and sustained balance and virtually indestructible! They are exquisite without any accompaniment, however, great company make them seem all the more enjoyable.

If Madeira were human, my husband may be concerned as I would be all over it... I LOVE Madeira wines.

IF A WINE WERE ME . . .
WHICH WOULD IT BE?

PORTS

STYLES OF	CHARACTERISTICS (ATTRIBUTES)	EXPRESSION (PERSONALITIES)	WINE STYLE (STYLE)	FINISH (DEMEANOR)
Dry, Semi-dry to Sweet	I am from Porto, Spain and have one luscious mouth-feel of deliciousness. You will find my adaptability suitable for all palate types. My grapes are usually a blend of different vintages bringing out the compilation of fruit, structure, acid and spice. You can find me aged to perfection or require decanting if Late Bottled Vintage, LBV and bottle age requirements for Vintage ports, but always intense of character and booze.	My extremely ripe grapes will usually trademark me when vinified, I'm meant to be drank young. When designed to age, as in a Tawny Port, you will find my fruits more concentrated and my flavors complex of nuts and roasted toffee... sophistication, that's me.	I am versatile as you can find me dry to sweet and all lusciousness in between. I am just as diverse with my colors, which range from white grapes to red. My confidence is acknowledged with subtleties and my vibrancy stays with you.	Delightfully engaging on any topic, I can be as easy going as you'd like, but you will always get my natural energy during discussions. I have been known to hang around in one's mind long after the conversation is over.

Food Styles of **Interest**: If with company, any and all will work. Assuming that you've chosen this wine to pair with food, identify which style will suit your meal best (Ruby or Tawny). Basic concepts to matching: wine acidity should exceed the food's acidity; the wine's residual sweetness should exceed the food's sweetness (the ruby port is going to be sweeter); and the weight of the food should match that of the wine (high alcohol will make the wines feel fuller). Considerations for a Ruby: This is really just fine as a sip by itself or with beautifully aged cheeses (cave aged blue) or chocolate and/or chocolate covered strawberries. For Tawny pairings (more nuttier flavors), go for bold cheeses, dried fruit and nut tarts.

I F A W I N E W E R E M E . . .

WHICH WOULD IT BE?

FORTIFIED WINE FEATURE - PORT / SANDEMAN

Why Port? Well Sandeman's Founders Reserve is not just any Port - it is one beautifully consistent-balanced **drink of perfection**.

This beauty is quite versatile whether on its own on the rocks or as a sexy cosmopolitan (a martini). Founders Reserve is one of Sandeman´s greatest Portos. selected from the finest lots of each vintage and aged for five years.

They have taken the wait out of it, as this Port is full of welcoming confidence, subtle complexity and ready to drink once bottled…So, *have at it!*

WHICH WOULD IT BE?

...Why Not?

Port is such a smooth drink and makes for a nice opening to any conversation - whether dry, semi-dry or sweet you really can't go wrong. And it pairs beautifully with one of the more difficult treats. Yes, chocolate! (yum)

When I attended a spectacular tasting with a nice line up of Sandeman Ports, it was pure bliss to sip through the myriad styles; The Founders Reserve seems to be perfectly suitable for any and all occasions. You just want to hang out with this drink. By just looking at the powerful red brilliant hues, your nose is extremely pleased with the bouquet of flowers and dark fruits that take you to another level. Imagine your palate being enveloped in the luscious black fruits, subtle spice, and a perfectly balanced vibrancy – and then finishing off with the ideal mix of intrigue and elegant mature poise...This is a drink of **great pleasure**!

I F   A   W I N E   W E R E   M E . . .

About **Sandeman**, founded in 1790 by George Sandeman, Sandeman Porto Founders Reserve is the culmination of two hundred years of expertise. These Porto wines are defined by their high quality and refined elegance, and their harmonious balance of acidity and structure. The winemaker, Luís Sottomayor, has a vision that is synonymous with the highest quality standards having learned from Fernando Nicolau de Almeida. Sottomayer guides the oenology team with solid technical expertise and refined cellar management skills, thanks to over 20 years of experience in the production, aging and blending of Porto Wines.

Find more about Sandeman wines: http://www.sandeman.eu/homepage/en

WHICH WOULD IT BE?

SHERRY

STYLES OF	CHARACTERISTICS (ATTRIBUTES)	EXPRESSION (PERSONALITIES)	WINE STYLE (STYLE)	FINISH (DEMEANOR)
Dry, Semi-dry, Medium sweet, Sweet	I am of Spanish origin, from Jerez, and only three grape varieties are allowed to create me (dependent on the style)...so realize the exclusivity you are embarking upon. I am developed with a nice protective yeast coat (flor) that helps to define my distinct flavors. I am often aged enough at bottling, revealing the complexities of the vintage blending process used to vinify me.	My flavors can show up from one extreme to the next based on your interest. I am known to be persistent with intense tanginess, nuts and dried fruit when dry. I offer a wide range of color from pale yellow to dark amber. When sweeter, I'm usually a blend of two varietals, PX and Muscat, with a dried fruit and fruit peel bitterness and very engaging on the palate.	Versatility is evident with me. I can be bold and intense in my dry structured form (Fino and Manzanilla) or sweet (PX/Muscat) or smooth and confident (Amontillado and Oloroso). You will know me by my distinct characteristics as I don't hide them regardless of how I'm vinified.	My conversations are always provocative and interesting. There is nothing simple with my discussions, so come prepared to be intrigued and offer up substance and then we will get along famously.

Food Styles of **Interest**: This is great company fully ready for conversation...sip and chat! Assuming that you've chosen this wine to pair with food, identify which style will suit your meal best (Manzanilla or Fino = dry, PX/Muscat = sweet, Amontillado = medium dry). Basic concepts to matching: wine acidity should exceed the food's acidity; the wine's residual sweetness should exceed the food's sweetness (PX/Muscat will be the sweetest style while Amontillado and Oloroso are semi-dry); and the weight of the food should match that of the wine.

Pairing considerations for the dry style include seafood, sardines, cured meats and milder cheeses as well as pickled garlic and olives. For the off-dry wine style, surprisingly BBQ, cured meats, poultry, and bold cheeses will work. For the sweet style, stick with bitter chocolate, bitter cheeses, and even a topping for ice cream sundae.

IF A WINE WERE ME . . .

WHICH WOULD IT BE?

VINS DOUX NATURELS / VDN

STYLES OF	CHARACTERISTICS (ATTRIBUTES)	EXPRESSION (PERSONALITIES)	WINE STYLE (STYLE)	FINISH (DEMEANOR)
Banyuls, Rivesaltes, and **Beaume de Venise**	I'm a lovely French fortified wine. and based on the region, I will be vinified of black or white varietals . Pleasant on the nose with a perfume scent, luscious ripened fruity goodness and balanced vibrancy. I am deceptively delicate taste - full body of concentrated fruits and texture will clarify my solid stance. When aged, you will notice more complexity of flavors imparted from the oak.	I can display multiple ways of being based on the type of varietal used Muscat will show off my sweeter delicate side vs. Grenache reveals my structure and vibrance. In either case, I will be energetic with acid and my natural sweet nature will always be in focus. I'm quite vocal of my styles and enjoyable to be around.	I can seem a bit outgoing with my style as I reveal all that I have to offer but done in good taste. I have interesting nuances about me and it takes a little time to decipher and understand.	My conversations are fully indulging and lingers with seductive details. You should be open to exploring as I will go the distance with my warm embrace and inviting discussion.

Food Styles of **Interest**: If with company, ensure they are worth it! Assuming that you've chosen this wine to pair with food, identify which style will suit your meal best. Basic concepts to matching: wine acidity should exceed the food's acidity (most will have active acidity); the wine's residual sweetness should exceed the food's sweetness (the sweetest style will have Muscat); and the weight of the food should match that of the wine (alcohol increases body in all sweet styles). Consider, then, sipping this as an aperitif or with a protein that's rich and savory. Certain hard salty cheeses will contrast and break down some of the opulent nature of these wines while nuts will bring that out in the wine.

WHICH WOULD IT BE?

VIN DE LIQUEUR

STYLES OF	CHARACTERIS-TICS (ATTRIB-UTES)	EXPRESSION (PERSONALI-TIES)	WINE STYLE (STYLE)	FINISH (DE-MEANOR)
Pineau de Charentes	I'm vinified in various regions throughout France and, while similar to a VDN, you will find that I'm a tad bit sweeter and can be a bit more boozy.	I am mostly about being embraced and enjoyed. I like entertaining and making the environment cozy and attractive. I am quite sweet natured and enjoy connecting with others.	I'm generally vinified sweet and seemingly cloying on occasion, but my acids are present and I'm quite boozy so balance the time hanging with me.	I am all about showering you with attention and comfort. I like to keep things pleasurable and make others feel good. My conversations are always enjoyable.

Food Styles of **Interest**: This is for good company looking for a great reason to relax and simply chill. When choosing this wine to pair with food, identify which style will suit your meal best. Basic concepts to matching: wine acidity should exceed the food's acidity); the wine's residual sweetness should exceed the food's sweetness; and the weight of the food should match that of the wine (alcohol increases body in all sweet styles). Pairing considerations include some Asian foods (Thai in particular with its light spice), shortbread cookies and fruit tarts. If red grapes were used to produce the vin de liqueur, chocolate covered fruits or flourless chocolate cake works well with the more bolder structure of the wine.

IF A WINE WERE ME . . .

WHICH WOULD IT BE?

FORTIFIED WINE FEATURE - VIN DE LIQUEUR / KARANTES

Why Vin de Liqueur? In a word, yum! There are varying styles of Vin De Liqueur, and those vinified with red grapes tend to have a notable structured profile. The one featured exemplifies the **delicacy in structure** with the use of 100% Grenache Noir grapes. The taste profile is inspiring with its stewed red fruits, pleasant acidity of limes with a hint of cocoa, concentrated dried figs and raspberries, spice and roasted almonds on a long velvety complex finish.

...Why Not? These types of wines can sometimes seem a bit too cloying, but the Karantes has done an amazing job producing this eloquent balanced **Karantes Vin de Liqueur**. It is a **drink for all senses**, with beautiful pale red hues, nose of roses, ripened red fruits, citrus peel, clove spice, and walnuts and almonds.

This is a beautiful bold wine of the Grenache variety, which is an ideal varietal given the soft tannins and naturally sweet fruit it possesses.

About the Winery

Château des Karantes is a magnificent vineyard named after the Bishop of Carcassonne and is situated in Languedoc-Rousillon, France. It is in the heart of a small valley near the Mediterranean. The estate offers a beautiful panoramic view of the Mediterranean Sea with the Pyrenees Mountains visible in the distance...romantic.

http://www.karantes.com/accueil.html

IF A WINE WERE ME...
WHICH WOULD IT BE?
NON-FORTIFIED WINES

SAUTERNES / LOUPIAC

STYLES OF	CHARACTERISTICS (ATTRIBUTES)	EXPRESSION (PERSONALITIES)	WINE STYLE (STYLE)	FINISH (DEMEANOR)
Other French regional styles... **Monbazillac, Quarts de Chaume, Sweet Vouvray**, etc	I'm from southern France, the known pedigree of white Bordeaux with my prestige of noble rot (fungus). I'm a blend of various different varietals filled with the most naturally concentrated flavors imaginable. My exquisite nature comes at a price because I'm required to be hand harvested, but I'm worth every bit being from Sauternes.	People associate me with premium quality and the finer things in life. I am a product of my influential upbringing, but enjoyable to be around and to entertain. My expression is of refined complexity with balanced vibrance, sweetness and structure ...I'm hard to be matched but other regions like Loupiac are outright opulently delightful.	I am versatile in my ways, but always of the highest caliber. I am all about quality; you will find many imitators that represent great taste but not the same quality. By coming from noble rot, there is always pronounced balanced richness flavors and texture.	My grape varietals create a complex discussion which marries nicely on the palate – though it's hard to pull any one thing out. The discussion lingers a long while and every aspect of it grows contagiously inviting.

Food Styles of **Interest:** If you want to impress your company, this is a great accompaniment to any aspect of your meal, whether savory or sweet. Assuming that you've chosen this wine to pair with food, identify which style will suit your meal best. Basic concepts to matching: wine acidity should exceed the food's acidity (all styles have medium to high acidity); the wine's residual sweetness should exceed the food's sweetness; and the weight of the food should match that of the wine (sweetness adds body / weight to wines).

For savory dishes, leverage rich flavors with cream sauces as a nice contrast of fatty proteins against the honeyed and textured wine. Elegant soft or hard blue cheeses break the luscious sweetness of the wine, and pair nicely with a nut based tart and dried bitter sweet fruits like apricots. Or, you can feel completely at ease having sips (chilled, of course!) without any pairings after a delicious meal.

TOKAJI ASZU

STYLES OF	CHARACTERISTICS (ATTRIBUTES)	EXPRESSION (PERSONALITIES)	WINE STYLE (STYLE)	FINISH (DEMEANOR)
Dry to Sweet to Syrupy sweet (Escenzia)	I'm world known for my sweet qualities yet I'm one of those rare secrets coming out of Hungary because the value placed on me. I am rare and deliciously complex with harmonized flavors of mandarin peel, honeysuckle, jasmine, and a luscious mouthfeel being of noble rot. The rigorous process to vinify me makes me an exclusive taste of wonderment.	I represent the finer things in life and am versatile with the common thread of rich concentrated fruit flavors and balanced energy, whether dry or syrupy sweet. As I mature, I'm expressed with more complexity, capturing the nuances of the six varieties permitted in making me.	I am perfectly balanced yet full of expression...you will see me a mile away. I love to flaunt my goodness from nose to palate and it's worth the experience. As I age, I am more intriguing to decipher, but you'll always have an amazing time with me.	Not ever forgotten...seriously! I am one of those memorable moments that continue to resonate long after the experience. I'm full of intrigue and passionate expression. Indulge consciously!

Food Styles of **Interest**: This is for interesting and curious people with a sophisticated palate, for sure. Assuming that you've chosen this wine to pair with food, identify which style will suit your meal best. Basic concepts to matching: wine acidity should exceed the food's acidity; the wine's residual sweetness should exceed the food's sweetness (Escenzia is incredibly sweet- the sweetest style); and the weight of the food should match that of the wine (alcohol will increase the body of the wines). Pairing considerations include nut based tarts and blue cheeses. Or, indulge freely without anything after a delicious meal (chilled)!

IF A WINE WERE ME . . .
WHICH WOULD IT BE?

VIN SANTO

STYLES OF	CHARACTERISTICS (ATTRIBUTES)	EXPRESSION (PERSONALITIES)	WINE STYLE (STYLE)	FINISH (DEMEANOR)
Dry to extremely sweet	I am mostly known in Tuscany Italy and my greatest strength is in my concentrated flavors. This comes from being harvested and then dried for some time (to evaporate moisture before fermentation), then aged for a minimum of three years.	I am known to be intriguing regardless of the style I am vinified. I tend to express confident maturity of raisiny fruits and nuts as I have age requirements after being fermented that help to contribute to my complexity and creamy finish.	I am a bold and diverse figure. You can find me completely dry and confrontational or a syrupy and cloying coating, gregarious in nature. My hues are just as diverse, from pale amber to a vibrant tawny orange.	My conversations can be heavy with intense substance or complimentary with a comforting touch - but never simple. My discussions extend for some time and always end with a smooth finish.

Food Styles of **Interest**: This is for good provocative company and best tasted after a nice meal. If a nibble is desired, assuming that you've chosen this wine to pair with food, identify which style will suit your meal best. Basic concepts to matching: wine acidity should exceed the food's acidity; and the weight of the food should match that of the wine. Considerations to try include cantuccini, dense small biscotti biscuits, fruit cake but with medium sweet style, flourless chocolate cake and pecan pie.

EISWEIN / ICEWINE

STYLES OF	CHARACTERISTICS (ATTRIBUTES)	EXPRESSION (PERSONALITIES)	WINE STYLE (STYLE)	FINISH (DEMEANOR)
In **Canada**, Vidal grapes are used to produce Icewine; whereby in **Germany** Riesling grapes are used.	I'm most notably known in Germany and Canada for my concentrated ripened flavors that are frozen on the vine. This captures my purest essence of acids and sugars during the long and slow fermentation, resulting in near perfect accuracy.	I like to think of myself as genuine and true to who and how I am naturally. I have a strong POV and am naturally and energetic balanced with my sweet fruitiness and lighter body. I belong to a small inner circle of likes, but love being appreciated by all.	My style is generally balanced of fresh sweet fruits of peach, pear and kiwi, and, depending on the varietal and vibrancy of the acid, I maintain a solid crispness.	You will find my conversations alive and pleasantly stimulating. I can seem a bit strong in my personality but balanced refection keeps the dialogue grounded. The discussion is deceptively light as the thoughts linger long after the talk begins. I am pleasingly stimulating.

Food Styles of **Interest**: This is for nice company that enjoy indulging in some exquisite decadence. Assuming that you've chosen this wine to pair with food, identify which style will suit your meal best. Basic concepts to matching: wine acidity should exceed the food's acidity; and the weight of the food should match that of the wine. Consider trying this wine after dinner with fruits or sorbet or cheeses (brie or aged, or smoked cheddar and Gouda).

IN CONCLUSION

We've now reached the end...but really it is just the beginning. What awaits you is a journey – a whole world of discovery with an unlimited array of flavors, aromas, textures, places, personalities, expressions, and relationships just waiting to be discovered. And you are the most essential part of it. As with people, all wines are unique and special in their own way.

While I have only been able to scratch the surface of the myriad wines, my hope is that it has piqued your interest in this fascinating (and delicious!) topic. So, go ahead get more curious. Discover some new wines and friends with common interests in wines. Whatever and however you choose to explore, I am delighted that you've shared in my passion and desire for you to have learned a little and enjoyed a lot.

- If you were intimated around wines in the past, I am excited that you now are a little more comfortable with understanding their different characteristics.

- If you never thought about wines as having personality or expression, hopefully you do now.

- If you like the way the wines were personified, perhaps you will remember what you like about a particular wine and therefore venture out to find other wines with similar expression.

- Hopefully you will have a chance to sample some of the wines featured here. Stay tuned for additional features in the next book (dare, I mention that, yes, there are several more books coming your way)!

FInally, while this book has, at times, challenged me to portray the true passion I have for wines and how they are expressed in writing, I hope that I've conveyed at least some of it to you and that it will inspire you to seek out new wines and new experiences.

I *thank you* for your indulgence.

I F   A   W I N E   W E R E   M E . . .
WHICH WOULD IT BE?

WINE PROFILE ASSESSMENT

"If A Wine Were Me.... Which Would it Be?", was inspired by Bwinedate.com, a service that connects wine enthusiasts with each other, both on-and off-line. So, if you found the book interesting, I encourage you check out Bwinedate to see about connecting with others who share an interest in wine.

As you have now read about the different varietals' expressions that are similar to you, you may be wondering just how accurate you are. Complete a short survey to find out for sure. Click on or paste the following link into your browser: https://novisurvey.net/n/wineprofile.aspx

Of course, you can also register as a member at www.Bwinedate.com to obtain a deeper level assessment as well as stay up to date on all of our wine events.

Salud, Salut, Santé and Cheers.

ACKNOWLEDGEMENTS

In what may seem like an odd delight, I wish to thank my mother, **Clara,** for always enlivening courage, spirit and belief in me. The legacy of her guiding principles course through me: achieve self-greatness, and always persevere with purpose and love in your heart...only now, am I able to see these principles with laser-focused lenses and find myself living with pure passion.

I would like to acknowledge my amazing teacher of ISG, **Aaron Sherman,** one of my greatest inspirations for enjoying learning and continuing my wine, spirits and beer studies. He made the topic fun for his students... was an animated and passionate teacher; even if you failed, he would have somehow turned it into an enjoyable experience for you (thank goodness I successfully passed the numerous grueling exams!). I'd also like to acknowledge author **Stephen Reiss** of *"Juice Jargon"* for starting me out with his book and availing himself as a mentor for me.

My devoted husband and fine artist, **Peter Georgeson,** deserves huge thanks, not just for his idea and contributions to the book and its cover art but for regularly listening to my many dreams, letting me babble on and on in my usual idea-flowing state of existence. Thank you to my great family for being there, particularly **Stephanie Green,** a writer herself, with her helpful contributions and support; **Linda Green** for her ideas, belief and encouragement of my studies -- *she* was the impetus for me writing a book, Jameliah Penfield and Yasmin Lashley. Thanks to my awesome friends for their unwavering support and belief in my dreams from self-reinvention: namely, **Jennifer Chhatlani** for her dedicated hard work and finessed editing and marketing of this book, **Linda Just** for her creative talents and book cover layout, Alicia Kan for her intense steering, Gina Elmore for all-around tremendous support, as well as Gentle Vuong, Lynn Evans McInnis, Skye Belline, Dawn Thomas, Rachel Morton, and Denise Mink...we are each other's forever fan club!

NOTEWORTHY CREDITS FOR BOOK

LaSaan Georgeson

If A Wine Were Me...Which Would it Be?
BOLD - SEXY - BUBBLY - SWEET

Edited by **Jennifer Chhatlani**
Cover art by **Peter Georgeson**

A special thanks to the following for their submissions:

Barboursville Vineyards, Benziger Family Winery, Château des Karantes, Cinder, Davis Family Vineyards, EFESTĒ Winery, Finca Decero Single Vineyard Wines, Gary Farrell Winery, Livon/ Tenuta RoncAlto, Sandeman's Port, Tempus Alba, Tenute Tomasella, The Rare Wine Co. and Vinhos Barbeito.

Made in the USA
Lexington, KY
15 October 2013